REVIEW

OF THE

Testimony given before the General Court Martial,

UPON THE TRIAL OF

BRIG. GENERAL GEORGE TALCOTT,

IN JUNE AND JULY, 1851;

AND OF

THE PROCEEDINGS OF THE COURT.

BY A COUNSELLOR AT LAW.

TO WHICH IS APPENDED

A COPY OF THE RECORD OF THE TRIAL.

ALBANY:
JOEL MUNSELL, 58 STATE STREET,
1851.

REVIEW

OF THE

Testimony given before the General Court Martial,

UPON THE TRIAL OF

BRIG. GENERAL GEORGE TALCOTT,

IN JUNE AND JULY, 1851;

AND OF

THE PROCEEDINGS OF THE COURT.

BY A COUNSELLOR AT LAW.

TO WHICH IS APPENDED

A COPY OF THE RECORD OF THE TRIAL.

ALBANY:
JOEL MUNSELL, 58 STATE STREET,
1851.

PREFATORY NOTE.

The reader of the following Review must not expect eloquence, or even the graces of composition. The subject is one of dry fact and drier law. There was no short and easy road to a conclusion in such a case. It presents an unusual mass of testimony requiring to be carefully scanned and compared; and there are intricate questions of evidence to be discussed. This could be done in a manner to satisfy the judgment of those sincerely disposed to arrive at the truth, only by a long and detailed examination of many minute circumstances and particulars. Hence the unexpected length of the article.

Although prepared in one sense, in a professional capacity, yet it is not the result of professional labor in the ordinary sense. It is the free, gratuitous offering of a friend of the accused, who, in common with thousands, was astonished at the verdict and sentence of the court; and who determined to satisfy his own mind, by the impartial exercise of his best faculties in a thorough examination of the case. Having done so, he deemed it a solemn duty to lay before the public, the grounds of his convictions. The result is before the reader. Gen. Talcott, whether able or not, will never be called upon for any compensation, nor will he be permitted to make any, but that of his good will and friendship.

The writer has not deemed it necessary to add his name to this Review. Desirous only to establish the truth and to maintain justice, he would have the facts and arguments he has exhibited speak for themselves, without the adventitious aid of any name, and without being prejudiced by it.

Some errors will be seen in the printed copy of the record of the trial. So far as they have been discovered, they are the errors of the manuscript copy furnished to Gen. Talcott.

REVIEW, &C.

If any apology be necessary for a calm, candid and thorough 1
examination of the evidence adduced on the trial of Gen. Talcott
and of the legal principles involved in the decision, it will be
found in the following considerations:

1. It is the first instance in our history of the dismissal of an
officer of his rank upon such charges, from a position regarded
in all services as of the highest importance; and it materially
affects the character of the nation, and particularly of the army.

2. It involves the reputation of an officer who for nearly forty
years had served his country in difficult and responsible stations,
faithfully, and with such success as to have received a brevet of 2
Brigadier General; and consigns his name and fame to undying
obloquy.

3. It also involves principles of law and practice, of the most
vital importance to every man bearing the commission of his
government in the army or the navy.

4. The case presents many minute facts and circumstances exceedingly complicated, in an unusual and irregular manner, so as
to require for the elucidation of the truth, all the skill to be derived from long experience in weighing testimony and great familiarity with the principles of legal evidence; qualities which it 3
would be absurd to expect from gentlemen devoted to the military
profession, and to duties quite unfavorable to a preparation for
the exercise of judicial functions.

5. A thorough and profound conviction, that the members of
the court martial, with the most upright intentions and with every
desire to do justice, have nevertheless misunderstood the testimony, or have mistaken altogether its force and bearing; have
disregarded (unintentionally) some of the elementary principles
of the law of evidence, and have rendered a verdict, which upon
careful retrospection, it is believed they will themselves regret. 4

Under such circumstances, this review is undertaken, for the
sake of justice, for the honor of the country and its military service, and to rescue, if possible, the fame of an innocent man from
undeserved reproach.

Disrespect to the members of the court, is not only utterly disavowed, but it is denied that it can justly be imputed to such an
5 investigation. The theory of our whole law, civil, criminal and
military, proceeds upon the principle that juries, judges and courts
martial may mistake the evidence, and misapply the law. The
decisions of the most distinguished judges of the courts, are every
day examined with the utmost freedom, and are often reversed.
The verdicts of the most intelligent juries, are daily canvassed
and scrutinized with unbounded license, and frequently set aside.

In a country where PUBLIC OPINION is the last and final arbiter
upon the proceedings of courts as well as the conduct of individuals, it is the right and indeed the duty of any citizen who after
6 deliberate examination believes that great injustice has been done,
even by a court martial composed of the most distinguished officers of the army, to submit his views of the grounds of its decision,
in a calm, dispassionate, respectful and manly appeal to the intelligence of his countrymen. The court martial which sentenced
Admiral John Byng to be shot, for not having done his utmost to
destroy the French fleet, was composed of the *elite* of the British
navy. And yet all historians concur in condemning their judgment.
One of the most accomplished of the number, Lord Mahon, writing
at the expiration of nearly a century after the event, declares that
7 while they were "swayed only by pure and honorable motives,"
yet that they committed a fatal error, and "confounded the two
ideas, neglect of duty, and error of judgment."* "Thus fell,"
says another historian, "to the astonishment of all Europe, Admiral John Byng; who, whatever his errors and indiscretions
might have been, seems to have been rashly condemned, meanly
given up, and cruelly sacrificed to vile considerations."† It is
not intended by this quotation to apply all or any of its epithets
to the case of Gen. Talcott, except that of rash condemnation.
It is believed that an error exactly like that described by Lord
8 Mahon, occurred in this case; that there was a confusion of the
ideas of "violation of duty" and "error of judgment." A patient and candid attention to the reasons for this conviction, is
solicited.

The public and private character of the accused, and his previous conduct in the public service, necessarily and justly form
elements of the greatest importance in the consideration of a
charge involving reckless and foolish insubordination, and the most
base duplicity, amounting to downright and repeated falsehoods,
without motive or object, and when the means of detection were
9 sure to be presented in claims for payment of the concealed work!
George Talcott, it appears from the army lists, was appointed 2d
lieutenant of the 25th regiment of infantry on the 10th day of
July, 1813. In August of that year he was transferred to the

---

* Lord Mahon's History of England, vol. 2, chap. 33,
† Smollett, vol. 2, chap. 6, sec. 46.

ordnance, and soon after was promoted to the grade of captain.
He served through the war, and on the re-organization of the corps 10
in August, 1832, was promoted at once to be lieutenant colonel. In 1839, although still only lieutenant colonel, he was called to Washington to take charge of the bureau as its chief; in this position he remained until 1840, when he was detailed to other services; but in February, 1842, was recalled to Washington, and continued to act as chief of the bureau, until on the decease of the colonel he was promoted to that grade in March, 1848. He remained in the same position during the Mexican war, and the value of his services was attested by the President and Senate
conferring on him the brevet of brigadier general. He continued 11
to serve in the same station until his arrest and condemnation by the court martial whose proceedings are the subject of the present enquiry.

During this long period of public service, thirty-eight years, and in different grades that he occupied as an ordnance officer, millions upon millions of public property have been in his charge, and millions of dollars of public money have been disbursed by him or under his direction, or subject to his examination; and not a trace is to be found of fraud, peculation, connivance with any contractor or dealer, waste, or even error in his accounts or in his
administration. Such is the public history of the man, condemned 12
upon charges whose atrocious character has been described. One who has known him for many years, intimately and thoroughly, and who knows his relatives, friends and companions, has the right to declare as he does, that in all the relations of life, the character of Gen. Talcott up to 1851, was not only untarnished, but that he was distinguished for a strict and rigid probity, not excelled by that of any living man.

Such a character, so earned, not in the absence of opportunity but amidst all the temptations and irregularities of ordinary service and the disorders of active hostilities, not only defies suspicion, but furnishes a shield and protection, in the minds of all 13
men capable of appreciating the difficulties of its attainment and its value, against the assaults of every thing but full, complete and overwhelming testimony. Let me not be misunderstood. In the investigation of truth, I scorn to invoke sympathy, which only disturbs the judgment. I rely on a principle of universal law and experience, that such a character, thus acquired, affords the strongest presumption, and is in itself evidence of the highest grade, against any charge which is grossly inconsistent with it. It proves the existence of settled principles and habits, without
which it could not have been attained. He who for forty years 14
has been trained in habits of subordination and obedience, can not at once and without motive, risk his commission and forfeit his reputation by a foolish and wanton defiance of positive orders. Some other explanation of any apparent incongruity of the kind, must be found. He who never uttered a falsehood in a life of

sixty-five years, the associate and companion of men of honor and
intelligence, can not have been guilty of a series of ridiculous
15 fabrications, without assignable motive, and which were sure of
inevitable detection in the ordinary course of his official business.
Such a tissue of absurdities in the conduct of a sane man, can be
rendered credible only by a strength of proof that would establish
a moral miracle.

In the preparation of this review, a difficulty has been experienced
in the strange and irregular manner in which the testimony
was introduced. Witnesses were not allowed to complete
their whole testimony, but were broken off and confined to matter
which the judge advocate deemed relevant to the particular charge
he was at the time prosecuting. Thus he constituted himself the
16 judge of the relevancy of every part of the evidence; and as
might be expected by any one familiar with judicial trials, matter
which qualified or explained what had been said or done, instead
of being found in juxtaposition with its subject, is scattered in
different and remote places, so that when read, its meaning and
bearing are not comprehended. No improper design is attributed
in adopting this mode of proceeding; nor any neglect of duty in
acquiescing in it. On both sides a spirit of accommodation appears,
and on the part of the defence, a confidence that no mode
of adducing the testimony could affect the accused. The refer-
17 ences to the various parts of the testimony, in this review, will
show how great a mistake was committed by such a departure
from a practice which is the result of ages of experience. And
to this cause may be attributed whatever misconception of evidence
and its bearing, may appear to have existed in the minds
of the court. This would have been remedied to a great extent,
if the usual custom had been observed by the judge advocate, of
summing up, classifying the testimony, presenting his theory of
the case, and the exact points of enquiry; which would have furnished
a thread to inexpert minds, through the mazes of desultory
18 and irregular testimony. I know not that it was his duty to do
this, unless required by the court; but I do say that our most
able and experienced judges are ever glad to have a case of any
complexity thus opened to them. And the omission in this case,
goes far to account for the result.

In the effort now made to classify the testimony, it has been
deemed useful to denote the *folios* by numeral figures in the margin,
so that when reference is made to a particular part, the designation
of it by the marginal number will enable the reader at
once to recur to the identical passage.

The FIRST CHARGE against Gen. Talcott (fol. 8), is "Vio-
19 lation of the 132d article of the regulations 'of the ordnance
department.'"

This must be founded on the 9th article of the rules and articles
of war, which declares that "any officer or soldier who shall *disobey*
any lawful command of his superior officer," shall suffer

death or such other punishment as a court martial may inflict.
There is no other article applicable to the charge. It obviously
implies something more than mere omission. Crime consists in 20
the intent. *Wilful* violation, would be disobedience. But simple
violation without any addition, can scarcely be called an offence,
because it may be accidental, involuntary. Every charge must
contain on its face and in itself an offence. This is not a mere
idle criticism. The second charge, which is of the same nature,
uses the important word that gives character to the act complained of, and alleges a "*wilful* disobedience." The difference
seems to indicate that the draftsman was conscious of the difficulty of establishing *intentional* violation of the regulation. If
the view now presented be correct, the charge should never have 21
been considered by the court, but should have been treated as a
fishing charge which might entrap. However innocently or igno-
rantly framed as a specimen either of ingenuity or negligence on
the part of the accuser, which meets us at the first step, it has
been deemed worthy of note.

The specification (fol. 8 to 14) does not support the charge:

1. It assumes that the regulation applies to the chief of the
ordnance department; and 2d, that it applies to order for open
purchase, and that none such can be made without previous
sanction by the Secretary of War.

The regulation will be found at folio 198. It forbids the mak- 22
ing of *contracts*, except by special authority of the chief of the
ordnance department, sanctioned by the Secretary of War; and
they are to be in triplicate, one of which is to be forwarded to
the chief. No reasoning seems necessary to show that it can not
by any fair construction apply to him who is to give the authority,
and to receive the contract. The subordinate officer who made
a contract under the special authority of the chief, but knowing
that it was not sanctioned by the Secretary, would violate the
regulation. It is obviously addressed to such and such only. It
does not either in terms or spirit forbid the chief giving the spe- 23
cial authority without the previous sanction of the Secretary.
Nor is there any necessity for such a construction. The colonel
of ordnance is an officer of the war department, and can do nothing without the express or implied authority of the Secretary.
This is a principle of law, not of regulation. And in this very
case of purchases, as well as contracts, the extracts from the laws,
folio 200, require that they *shall be made* under the *direction* of
the Secretary of War. It would be worse than a work of super-
erogation, to repeat a law in a regulation. If Gen. Talcott authorized an open purchase or a contract, without the direction of 24
the Secretary, he violated the law, not the regulation.

For this, he was not put upon trial. But it will be shown
hereafter, that if he had been, or if the regulation be deemed to
extend to him, the proof is abundant to establish that such a
direction was given.

2. Nor does the regulation apply to *open* purchases. The distinction between them and contracts, is recognized in article
25 8 of the same regulations (see folio 208): "Ordnance and ordnance stores shall be provided by open purchase, by fabrication, or by contract, as may be most advantageous, &c." It was well understood and recognized in practice by the Secretaries (see fol. 455, 459). They are reported separately to the head of the department (folio 217).

Their being sometimes called contracts and sometimes orders (215) in ordinary speech or letters, can not be allowed to change the precise terms of a regulation. But if the phrase "contracts" was really susceptible of two meanings, surely no officer can be
26 inculpated for having adopted one of those meanings.

Now it is only necessary to look at the order of 6th November, 1850, (folio 9, 10,) to see that it was for an open purchase. And it is not pretended that it assumed any different character subsequently. Col. Huger never reduced it to the form or essence of a contract.

If then, the truth of the specification were admitted, it does not sustain the charge, because in giving an order for an open purchase, no contract was made, and because the regulation did not include the chief of the ordnance bureau; both of which are assumed by the charge.

27 But the specification is not proved. The two facts upon which it proceeds are, 1, that the order was without the sanction of the Secretary; and 2, that Gen. Talcott allowed and approved a contract which Col. Huger made with Carmichael (fol. 13).

1. What is meant in the regulation by "*the sanction* of the Secretary," or in the law by "the *direction* of the Secretary?" Surely, in the multifarious concerns of that branch of the service, it could not have been intended that the express, immediate and direct sanction and authority of the Secretary should be given to all its minute transactions.

The relations of the chief of the ordnance bureau and of the
28 chiefs of all the other bureaus to the Secretary of War are analogous to those of the Secretary with the President. From the nature of the case, each must possess a general discretionary authority in the execution of the details of the business confided to them. This in respect to the Secretaries has been often decided by the Supreme Court. The authority of the chiefs of bureaus must be implied from a general sanction by their immediate superior of any plan or project submitted to him. Thus, Secretary Marcy informs us of the usage in the war department that when estimates for a particular service were submitted to and approved
29 by the Secretary, and appropriations made, the bureau went on, without being required to apply for further particular directions, and expended the money. "I suppose," he says, "the head of the bureau considered that he had my consent, as I had approved the estimates; I do not mean to say that I did not expect to be

consulted, as the appropriations were sometimes very general"
(folio 454). Here the usage is established, that the approbation
of the estimates was considered a *consent* that the bureau should 30
go on and execute them. This was the *sanction.* Whether the
Secretary was to be afterwards *consulted* or not, that is advised
with, depended on the circumstances, as when the appropriations
were very *general.* But this was a question of expediency and
propriety. The omission to consult, could not affect the previous
consent and sanction, much less rescind it.

Now, it appears from the executive documents No. 1, of the 1st
session 31st Congress, page 123, that Gen. Talcott as chief of the
ordnance bureau, submitted an estimate of the funds required for
the service of the ordnance department for the fiscal year com-
mencing 1st July, 1850, amounting to $100,000; and remarks 31
among other things as follows: "The appropriations will be
applicable to the procurement of sea coast and garrison artillery,
projectiles, timber, stone and other materials," &c. This is dated
October 17, 1849, and was transmitted to Congress by the Secretary of War, and thereby adopted and sanctioned by him. The
estimate thus submitted was approved by Congress, and an appropriation of $100,000 made in pursuance thereof (see *Laws of*
U. S., 1st session 31 *Congress, p.* 506). Again on the 15th October,
1850, Gen. Talcott submitted another estimate of appropriations
required for the service of his bureau for the fiscal year com- 32
mencing July 1, 1851, for $200,000. The same remark was made
as to the purposes to which the appropriation would be applicable,
viz: "the procurement of sea coast and garrison artillery, *pro-*
jectiles, timber, iron, &c." This was transmitted by the Secretary of War to the Secretary of the Treasury, and by the latter
laid before Congress in his report of December 2, 1850. These
estimates thus sanctioned were in full force on the 6th of November, 1850. As to one of them, an appropriation had been made;
as to the other it was not expected, and in the ordinary course of
legislation would not be made until the close of the session. In 33
fact the appropriation bill for the support of the army passed on
the 3d March, 1851, (*p.* 620 *Laws of 2d session* 31*st Congress*).
Whether the whole or any part of this last estimate was appropriated or not, is not now material. We are enquiring into the
state of things on the 6th of November, 1850, and whether the
Secretary had at that time sanctioned estimates for projectiles.
Orders for them would necessarily be prospective, and dependent
on the appropriations. If none were made, the orders would of
course be modified, or rescinded. That the Secretary of War
sanctioned the procurement of ordnance supplies, including pro- 34
jectiles, to a large amount, by approving the estimates, is evident.
But in point of fact there was an appropriation in the act of
March 3, 1851, p. 620, "for the purchase of ordnance, ordnance
stores and supplies, one hundred thousand dollars." And this,
according to the testimony of Capt. Maynadier, a witness for the

prosecution, was applicable to the purchase of "suitable projectiles" (folio 46).

35 It is submitted then, that the order of 6th November, 1850, is brought entirely within the usage and understanding of the department as proved by Secretary Marcy. At all events, the usage and practice is sufficient to exonerate Gen. Talcott from any charge of *wilful* violation of the regulation, in conforming to that usage. And now it may be perceived why *the charge* omitted to apply the term "wilful" or any other criminating epithet to the "violation" complained of.

In addition to all this, the prosecutor has himself admitted the fact. He knew whether he had *sanctioned* and generally or otherwise authorized an order for the open purchase of shot and shells.
36 On the 27th of January, 1851, a copy of this order of 6th November, 1850, was received by him from Gen. Talcott, and he says, (folio 291):

"This answer being perfectly satisfactory, I ceased to think on the subject, until my attention was again called to it a short time after by Mr. Green, when it occurred to me that possibly Col. Huger might be making shot under that order of the 6th November." Whatever was done by Col. Huger under the order, could not affect the question of fact, whether the order itself was or was not authorized. With the issuing of the order, he was perfectly satisfied. But without dwelling on the words used by
37 him, it is enough to say that the very omission to negative any authority to issue the order, when it was first presented to his notice, and when he was bound to speak, was in itself a recognition of its being authorized. It is true that in his testimony on a subsequent day (folio 388), he says he did not then know that there was a regulation, requiring the sanction of the Secretary to all contracts. This was after he had been some six months in office! But even this ignorance will not avail. He knew that as head of the department, responsible for all its expenditures, he must have the control of them; and he certainly knew the
38 law of Congress which required that sanction.

The 2d question of fact on which the specification is founded, viz., that Gen. Talcott allowed and approved the contract as it is called, subsequently made by Col. Huger, it is not necessary now to discuss; because the authority being shown its extent is immaterial under this charge. And that question is so prominent in the subsequent charges, that it must necessarily be discussed when they are considered.

This first charge is apparently so unimportant when compared with those that follow, that it may be supposed more time and
39 consideration have been given to it than it deserved. But it was evidently regarded by the prosecutor as the foundation of the superstructure he was about to raise. If the charge of a gross and palpable violation of a fundamental printed regulation with which he was as well acquainted as with his alphabet, could be

fastened upon an old soldier, the ice would have been broken, and the court would be prepared to listen with more complacency to other charges, which if presented at once in all their deformity, might shock credulity and produce a revulsion unfavorable to 40
the prosecution. Without assigning motives, which is not my province, I have a right to speak of tendencies and natural consequences of acts. Common sense as well as law draws the conclusion.

The singular form of the charge; the attempt to stretch the regulation so as to cover an officer and a case not within its plain import; the confounding the regulation with the law; the denial of a previous sanction and directions which had been given according to the usage of the department; and above all, the implied admission of that sanction by the prosecutor's silence when the order was made known to him and his declaration of satis- 41
faction with it, not only show that the facts and law under this charge could not have been understood by the members of the court, when they found the accused guilty of it; but they are important as leading events and circumstances in the history of the case to exhibit the *animus* which dictated the prosecution.

The SECOND CHARGE (fol. 14 to 18) is *wilful* disobedience of orders and instructions, and it is founded upon specifications which allege these facts:

1. That the Secretary of War made a decision, which was known to the accused, refusing to make *any* contract with Car- 42
michael; and 2. That the accused notwithstanding, by his letter of November 6th, intended to authorize and procure a contract for Carmichael, and subsequently allowed and sanctioned a contract made with C. by Col. Huger.

1. Did the Secretary decide at the interview with Carmichael, that he should not have *any* contract for shot? or did he merely reject his claim to a confirmation of an alleged previous understanding for a contract? The evidence of the prosecutor on this point is given in folios 60 to 67; what follows is wholly irrelevant to this question of fact. Down to the question at folio 66 (printed 96), not a word passed, but what related to Carmichael's claim 43
for a recognition of his contract or agreement for a contract; except the statement that "the Dr. made a very earnest appeal to me to be allowed to make some shot," and presented arguments to induce the Secretary to allow him to make some shot. This would appear at first sight as if C. had applied for a new order. But this impression is removed by the Secretary's answer: "But I *persisted* in my refusal in very positive terms, and he left the office somewhat dissatisfied at my decision." The phrase here used *persist*, imports a repetition or continuance in something that had been previously said or done. We look in vain for any 44
thing previously in reference to a new or original order or contract, but the whole conversation related to the claim for recognition of an old contract. Again, he speaks of it as a *decision*,

the appropriate term for a judgment upon a claim; but not so appropriate for the refusal of a request for a new favor.

The question which the judge advocate immediately put, indi-
45 cates his consciousness that as yet the Secretary had said nothing about a refusal of *any* contract or order; and he seeks to draw out some reason assigned at the time, that would be so general as to apply to a new contract or order, and authorize the inference that such a one had also been interdicted.

And now the Secretary says, "*My impression* is, and it is very strong, that I stated to him that the department was not at that time in want of shot, or was not making shot; on that point, however, I will not be positive." And this the writer avers is every syllable in the testimony of the prosecutor, that has any
46 reference whatever to the point in dispute, viz., whether the Secretary decided that Carmichael should not have *any* contract for shot. So that this *impression* of which he will not be positive, is the sole foundation for the allegation that a *decision* was made, amounting to "orders and instructions" (folio 17), which the accused *wilfully* disobeyed.

The real and true point of the only enquiry which the specification authorized, and which has already been stated, is so obscured by irrelevant matter about Gen. Talcott's having a bundle of papers and not thrusting them in the Secretary's face before he was even asked about them, and about his not confirming by
47 an impertinent interference the decision of his superior, that it is not at all surprising that the court were bewildered and suffered an impression to be made on their minds by circumstances so skillfully interwoven with the lame and impotent evidence bearing on the real point of enquiry, and which if it had been left in its nakedness, would have excited only merriment at such a foundation for such a charge.

But this is not all. The prosecutor has himself furnished evidence that he did not regard the decision on Carmichael's claim, as a refusal and instruction that he should not be permitted to furnish *any* shot. At folio 389 he gives his reasons for issuing
48 the order of 29th January, 1851, which will be found at folio 266, and proceeds to say: "when I had the conversation with Gen. Talcott and learned that shot was making, and being at that time ignorant at what *time* the contract had been made, I supposed it possible it had been made since the adoption of that regulation (of 29th January), and *that* was the disobedience I referred to." This testimony is given to explain what he had said to Gen. Talcott in the presence of Mr. Anderson (fol. 388). He had then said (fol. 333), "the question now was simply, whether *an order* of *the department* had been obeyed by its officers," &c. This
49 conversation was after the 19th of April, (see fol. 311,) the date of Gen. T.'s letter. Now it will be seen, that he was then fully informed by Mr. Anderson, that he had made shot "under a contract which was made by Dr. Carmichael with Col. Huger" (fol.

335). He knew as well at that time as he did at the drawing up
of the charges and specifications, all the facts and circumstances
of the order to Huger of Nov. 6, and of Huger's arrangement with
Carmichael, and that shot had been made and sent to Fort Mon- 50
roe under it. At this time and with this knowledge, he does not
pretend that there had been any disobedience of his *decision* not
to permit Carmichael to make *any* shot; but the disobedience of
which he complained, was the supposed violation of a peremptory
written order made on the 29th of January. Can there be any
evidence more satisfactory than this, that the Secretary did not
suppose he had made any decision, or given any instructions forbidding any order whatever to, or any contract with Carmichael,
which Gen. Talcott had violated?

Under other circumstances, it might be proper to enquire when, 51
how and why, this change of ground was made, by which, when
the order of 27th January turned out to be *after* the alleged offence, a supposed *decision* of a prior date was invoked. But it is
unnecessary.

After this testimony there follows an extraordinary series of
questions and answers, occupying nearly two pages from folio 67
to 74, not one word of which has the least bearing upon the question of fact as to the extent of the Secretary's decision. They
are occupied in showing that Gen. Talcott did not contradict
Carmichael when he alleged that Secretary Crawford had recognized his contract; that Gen. T. remained silent when Mr. Con- 52
rad conclusively refuted Carmichael's claim; that before Mr.
Conrad had said any thing, Gen. T. did not take out of the bundle of papers he had brought with him, the letter of Secretary
Crawford and hand it to the Secretary; and that afterwards he
told the prosecutor he was "right, there never was any recognition of the contract." What possible bearing had any one or all
these incidents, upon the question of fact, what decision had been
made as to Carmichael's having any future order or contract?
The prosecutor calls it an "accidental circumstance" (folio 67),
that he called for the papers to sustain a claim made to him, 53
founded in part on those papers which had been referred to, and
were then in his sight! The burthen of his complaint seems to
be, that he would have been beguiled and entrapped into the
sanction of a worthless claim, if he had not possessed the extraordinary sagacity that dictated an enquiry for the paper on which
the claim was founded. And this dangerous trap he explains in
his own peculiar way.

The different versions of this trap which he has given, are
worth pursuing, in this episode which he introduced for purposes
but too visible. Folios 67, 68, he says, "I should have taken
the fact as certain, [the fact that Secretary Crawford had recog- 54
nized the claim,] being, as I am, in the habit of receiving as evidence of fact every *report* and *statement* made to me by the head
of a bureau." When it appeared from the cross-examination of

the witness (folio 70), that Gen. Talcott had not said one word during the interview, except in answer to a question of the Secretary, that the bundle in his hand were the papers he enquired
55 for, and that, therefore, there could have been neither *report* nor *statement* by him, he changes his reason, and says, (folio 73,) "as I have stated, I am in the habit of receiving the *declarations* or *admissions* of heads of bureaus with implicit confidence."

Being again pressed with a question, he says at folio 74, that he considered the *silence* of Gen. Talcott, when Carmichael asserted the recognition by Mr. Crawford, "as *equivalent* to making the declaration himself or *nearly so*"—a singular qualification and a strange inference! We have still another version of his views on the subject. At folio 85, he says, "I had supposed it
56 *possible* that Gen. Talcott agreed with Dr. Carmichael in supposing that Mr. Crawford's letter amounted to a recognition of the contract."

From a *report* or *statement* (fol. 67, 68), it dwindled down into *declarations* or *admissions* (fol. 73), and then again, into a *silence*, equivalent to a declaration or *nearly so* (fol. 74), and then it passes off into a thin vapor of a *possibility* (fol. 85).

If there be any thing ludicrous in this specimen of bathos, it is not the fault of the reviewer. He has added no colors to those furnished by the prosecutor's pallet. There was no charge or specification of Gen. Talcott's having endeavored to deceive the
57 Secretary into the belief of the fact asserted by Carmichael, that Secretary Crawford had recognized his claim. And therefore the whole of this fanfaronade was impertinent to the issue, illegal, and in any civil court of justice would have been peremptorily excluded. But being admitted and spread on the record, its value as evidence of any thing required to be weighed. The object, or rather the effect of its introduction, upon minds unaccustomed to the analysis of evidence, is but too palpable.

If then it has been established, as I trust it has, that the proof utterly fails to show that the Secretary made a *decision*, which
58 amounted to instructions and orders, forbidding *any* order to or contract with Carmichael for shot; and that on the contrary the evidence rebuts the idea of any such decision, then this charge might be dismissed at once, as being destitute of the very first and most essential ground for its support. But, as it is intended in this review not to leave a single point unexplored, an examination of the *second* ground on which this charge rests, will be made. That ground is, assuming that instructions had been given by the Secretary, not to give any order or make any contract with Carmichael for shot, Gen. Talcott did notwithstanding, by his letter of Nov. 6, intend to authorize and procure a contract
59 for Carmichael to deliver a large quantity of shot, and subsequently allowed and sanctioned a contract made with him for that purpose by Col. Huger.

The importance of this accusation in considering the subsequent charge, if not in the discussion of this, demands a patient attention to details, in order to ascertain the precise truth of the case.

It is evident that the essence of the charge consists in the supposed procuring and subsequent sanction of a contract for *a large* 60
quantity of shot. The prosecutor has not complained of the order of November 6, if it can fairly be regarded as an order for the open purchase of a small or limited quantity. It is by connecting that order, in the specification and in the evidence, with the subsequent arrangement of Col. Huger by which 500 tons of shot were ordered (fol. 11, 17), that criminality is given to it. Hence our attention must be directed exclusively to that arrangement of Col. Huger, and we are to enquire whether Gen. Talcott intended to procure it to be made, and whether he sanctioned it?

Preliminary to examining that order of November 6, it is proper 61
to notice a previous letter, which is alluded to by Col. Huger at folios 446, 447, where he gives what he supposed to be its substance. The letter itself has since been found and lodged in the war department. The following is a copy of it, as furnished to the counsel of Gen. T.:

ORD. DEPT., 1 Nov. 1850.

My dear Colonel—

Dr. Carmichael is very much in want of a contract for shot. Do you want any 42 pound or 32 pd. shot, and if so how many? The returns from your post show 5,725 of the first and 28,450 of
the latter. 62

Yours truly,

G. TALCOTT.

The answer to this letter is given at folio 260. In it Col. Huger says from the number of guns to be mounted of 32 pounders, after deducting what shot were on hand 33,550 or nearly 500 tons, would be *required*. This is in answer to the enquiry how many were *wanted*.

Upon the receipt of this letter, the *order* of November 6 as it is called, but rather the *authority* of that date, was given (fol. 9,
289). It requires careful examination. It says, "It may be *well* 63
to provide more shot and shells from *time to time*"—"and for this purpose you are authorized to procure them to a *reasonable extent*." "You will make the necessary *estimates* of funds to meet the deliveries as they occur; they should be procured by *open purchase* only."

It must be evident to the most superficial observer, that this authority did not meet Col. Huger's opinion of what was required. Instead of 500 tons, he might procure shot to a *reasonable extent*. And to that extent, not at once by a binding contract, but from
time to *time* by open purchase. The very expression, from time 64
to time, means, as the exigencies of the post required. Intervals of duration are denoted by the phrase. It is the common elipti-

cal expression for occasion, necessity. The physician administers
his medicines from time to time; the baker supplies me with
bread from time to time; it would be a pleonasm to add, as cir-
65 cumstances required, or as I wanted bread, because every one
would so understand the phrase. Col. Huger's quiet suggestion
that there was room to place 500 tons, and that "they would be
in a convenient position to be transported elsewhere if required,"
thus insinuating the propriety of procuring that quantity, even if
not wanted at Fort Monroe,—was lost upon Gen. Talcott. He
will not order such a quantity, but authorizes the procurement
to a limited extent of what might be wanted, as the occasion required.

That this is the fair construction which any intelligent man
would give to this order, is proved by a very competent witness
66 produced by the prosecutor. Capt. Maynadier (fol. 442) says,
"I always supposed and frequently mentioned to Gen. Talcott
that Col. Huger had in my opinion exceeded his instructions of
the 6th of November in giving the order to Dr. Carmichael, and
that his conduct in giving that order was to me totally inexplicable." This was the view taken by a gentleman conversant with
the course and practice of the bureau, and entirely disinterested.

The prosecution has also introduced as evidence, the declaration of the accused. By every rule of evidence and common justice he is entitled to the benefit of whatever is contained in such
67 declarations that may benefit him while he is to be affected by
what may militate against him. His adversary has made him a
witness, and can not object to his testimony. The answer of
Gen. Talcott to the minute enquiries of the Secretary of War, is
given at large (fol. 374 to 387). It is a frank manly statement
of all he did or knew in reference to the transaction. At folio
381 he says, "He (Col. Huger) never told me that he wished to
give any man a contract, and when I heard that Carmichael had
one for 500 tons, I scouted the idea, taking for granted that no
officer of my corps could so misconstrue authority to make 'open
purchases' of shot, or could convert my letter of the 6th Novem-
68 ber, into authority to give such an order."

Further comment on the meaning of this order, is deemed quite
unnecessary. But some stress seems to have been laid upon Gen.
T.'s letter of November 1, already given (fol. 61 above). It was a
mere letter of enquiry to know if there was any exigency or occasion for any shot, beyond the quantity reported as on hand.
There could have been no design in writing it, to draw out an
answer which would furnish an excuse for a future order in favor
of Carmichael for a *large quantity* of shot; because although such
an excuse was furnished by Col. Huger's answer, Gen. Talcott
69 refused to avail himself of it as we have already seen.

Evidence was adduced that Col. Huger had a general authority
to procure shot for experiments (fol. 438, 447), for the purpose
doubtless of raising a suspicion that the letter of November 6

really meant more than it purported, and was intended to authorize the procurement of a large quantity of shot. The explanation given by Gen. Talcott (fol. 376), to give "Carmichael *a* 70
chance to make a bargain if he could for *some shot and shells*," which was called for and produced by the prosecution, affords a rational and natural explanation for his reiterating an authority already possessed by Huger. It pointed Col. Huger's attention to Carmichael as one whom Gen. T. was willing to oblige. And this was the precise effect it had on Col. Huger, who says, at folio 175, in answer to the question "*how* came the order to be given to Carmichael?" "because *he* brought it to me was one reason."

Gen. T. doubtless felt some compassion for Carmichael who had been so grievously disappointed in the rejection of his claim, 71
and in the kindness of his heart was willing to aid him in doing a small job—to a limited extent—at the works in which he had been known to be interested.

It is supposed then, to be evident that the letter of November 6, cautiously avoided sanctioning the procurement of the large quantity of shot which Huger had indicated, while it answered the purpose of avoiding the importunities of Carmichael. Of the *prudence* of writing any letter whatever on the subject, I have nothing to say. He was not upon trial for want of it. But the main fact on which the specification under this charge rests, is that Gen. Talcott subsequently approved the order given by Col. 72
Huger to Carmichael. Although this point becomes unimportant in the consideration of this second charge, if it be established that there was no decision, instruction or order of the Secretary forbidding an order to or contract with Carmichael, yet as it is fairly presented here and is so controlling in the consideration of the remaining charge and its specifications, it is proposed to bestow upon it a careful consideration.

It is not pretended that there was any formal official approval or sanction of the order to Carmichael, but one is attempted to be inferred from circumstances supposed to prove knowledge of 73
that order and of its being in the course of execution, and an acquiescence in such execution. The exact point is here stated with great care, and it is essential to the proper appreciation of the case that it should be understood and seen to be fairly stated. Knowledge of the order to Carmichael, if that order had become a dead letter and was not put in force, would be nothing. It was its execution, the deliveries of shot under it, a knowledge of that fact, and an acquiescence by Gen. Talcott in such execution, that constitute the offence as attempted to be proved.

It may be observed that acquiescence in not arresting the pro- 74
ceeding of a subordinate officer, is not necessarily an approval or sanction of that proceeding. And it might well be urged that if the very fact claimed to be proved, were established, namely, acquiescence, it does not support the specification which charges

approval and *sanction*. But no such narrow ground will be taken
in this review. The spirit of the charge shall be met directly,
75 exactly as it was intended.

As there could be no sanction or approval of any proceeding
without knowledge of its existence, the question is reduced to the
single enquiry, whether Gen. Talcott after the letter to Mr. Kemble of November 21, 1850, (folio 101,) knew that Anderson was
fabricating shot and delivering large quantities at Fort Monroe
under the order of Col. Huger to Carmichael? The prosecution
hold the affirmative of this enquiry and are bound to maintain it.
And it is insisted that this must be done by the most satisfactory
and conclusive proof, under the circumstances stated in the preliminary remarks of this review. In a remark of the judge advo-
76 cate at folio 114, we have an indication of one part of the evidence
on which he relied to establish this knowledge and approval, viz:
"the whole matter referred to witness (Huger) and entrusted to
him with approval of his objections to a transfer of the contract."
This refers to the testimony contained between folios 95 and 105,
in which is related the reference of Kemble's letter to Col. Huger,
that he might answer it, as he gave the order. Had Gen. Talcott known of the arrangement of Huger with Carmichael, he
could himself have answered Kemble's letter. And the fact of
its reference to Huger to be answered is presumptive evidence
77 that Gen. T. knew nothing about the matter. "The whole matter" was not referred to Huger, nor was it "entrusted to him,"
but it was sent to him for a specific and proper purpose. But
the approval of Huger's objections to the transfer of the contract,
is urged as evidence of an approval of the contract or order to
Carmichael itself. Let that letter at folio 101 be read, and to
any one willing to understand words in their ordinary sense, it
will appear that it repudiates any such contract as Kemble had
said Carmichael informed him he had made with Huger. To
understand it fully, it should be observed that Mr. Kemble was
78 well known to be the proprietor of a large iron establishment
opposite West Point on the Hudson river, capable of fabricating
the whole quantity of 500 tons in a few months, as he intimated
in his letter (folio 99), that it would employ his moulders during
the winter. Now, Huger's letter to Kemble says (folio 102),
that it was understood the work was to be done at Carmichael's
foundry, "which *could* only turn them out in *limited quantities as
required*, and as I had means to pay for them." This was a denial
of the representation that such a quantity had been absolutely
ordered. The whole amount that might be ultimately required
79 was stated, Huger says, to enable Wellford, the partner of Carmichael, to make his calculations and arrangements for materials
(fol. 103). But the whole was limited to be furnished as thereafter
required, and as he should be furnished with means to pay for
them. And therefore, he would not consent to the transfer of

the order to Carmichael, in the *manner* he had proposed to Kemble. What is here meant is evident; the *manner* was an unrestricted transfer of what Carmichael represented as an absolute 80
and unconditional order to a foundry that would immediately execute it. So far as the letter of Huger described the order to Carmichael, it was substantially what Gen. Talcott had authorized (folio 9), to provide shot and shells from time to time to a reasonable extent, and to be founded on estimates, through which Huger would be furnished with "means to pay for them," as he said in his letter to Kemble.

Why should not Gen. T. approve of such a letter? It met directly the enquiry of Mr. Kemble, and it repudiated utterly the representation of Carmichael. It was Col. Huger's affair, not 81
his. It was sufficient to satisfy him as the superior officer, that an effectual stop had been put to Carmichael's attempted transfer. The matter in hand was disposed of. What more could he require to be inserted in the letter to Mr. Kemble, a private gentleman, not an officer of the government?

Col. Huger's statement of the nature of his arrangement with Carmichael, is confirmed by Capt. Stone (folio 106), who says that Carmichael "said most expressly that he wanted the contract for the sole purpose of starting the foundry" called Wellford's; and he reiterates the same at folio 370. It is sworn to 82
by Col. Huger (fol. 349, 350).

The remark of Col. Huger, that the shot were to be turned out in limited quantities as required, and as he had means to pay for them, explains any apparent indifference in respect to the order given to Carmichael, which Gen. Talcott manifested. The shot were to be paid for on delivery (fol. 10, fol. 12); these payments could only be made by funds obtained by estimates (fol. 10), which must of course precede the delivery. If an estimate came to the bureau for a quantity larger than intended to be authorized, the bureau had the means of instantly stopping the delivery by refusing to supply the estimated funds. Thus Gen. Talcott had 83
complete control of the whole business, and if Col. Huger had exceeded his instructions, it could be disavowed, and would be disavowed when information of such excess reached the bureau through the estimates. Gen. Talcott might therefore feel perfectly at ease in respect to any apprehension of the government being encumbered with an undue quantity of shot and shells. There was no occasion for him to make any stir or noise about it; he held the check string in his own hands.

It is evident that when the judge advocate says (folio 115), that the order to Carmichael was not repudiated, he refers in 84
part to the manner in which Gen. Talcott spoke to Col. Huger about it, when first apprised of the fact (folio 104). Col. H. says: "He also did express surprise at the *amount* of the order; but I did not understand him as *reproving* me for giving an order

[not*] in compliance with his instructions." In examining the testimony of this witness, it should not be forgotten that his own
85 conduct was under enquiry, and that he was under a strong temptation to exonerate himself by transferring as much of the censure attached to the transaction, to his superior officer, as possible. The influence of this temptation is very visible in the great difference between the account he *first* gave to the Secretary of War, when called upon for an explanation of the affair, and that which he gave as a witness under oath and in presence of Gen. Talcott. Will the reader turn to folio 339 and read the statement made by Col. H. on his *ex parte* and *private* examination. He says: "A few days after the order was given, witness
86 came to this city and informed Gen. Talcott of the order he had given Carmichael; does not recollect that Gen. T. said anything in particular when he communicated the fact to him." And at folio 344 he says, he "never communicated to General Talcott *officially* the order he had given to Carmichael; he informed him of it, however, *privately*, as above stated." The impression produced by such statements would be that he had privately and in a manner to avoid its appearance on the files of the department, apprised Gen. Talcott *how* his letter of November 6 had been carried into execution, and that no disapprobation or even sur-
87 prise was expressed by Gen. T., and therefore it was silently approved. And such *was* the impression made on the mind of the Secretary. See folio 336, where he says, "From this statement (Huger's) it would seem that you were apprised of the order to Carmichael to make five hundred tons of shot, a few days after it was given, and that you *approved* of it." Now, will the reader turn to folio 97 and see the account of the same transaction given under oath. Huger arrived in Washington after the 17th of November, the date of Kemble's letter; instead of *his* informing Gen. Talcott of the order to Carmichael privately, that informa-
88 tion was already possessed by Gen. T. by means of Kemble's letter; and instead of his volunteering to tell what he had done, it was drawn from him by a reference to him of Kemble's letter. And this was the *first* occasion of consultation between them on that subject (folio 101). How very different is the aspect of the transaction now presented! But further; Col. Huger, in his examination by the Secretary, "does not recollect that Gen. T. said any thing in particular, when he communicated the fact to him." Now, turn to folio 104, where the same gentleman *swears* that Gen. Talcott remarked that the Secretary would be justly
89 incensed; and expressed *surprise* at the *amount* of the order. Surely here was something, very particular.

Now, when we consider even his testimony under oath, it is

---

* The word "not" is not in the copy of the record furnished Gen. Talcott. But it is manifest some negative is necessary to the witness's meaning. He could not well be reproved for giving an order in compliance with instructions.

evident allowance must be made for his situation and the effect it
would naturally have on his memory. What he might regard as
merely *surprise*, may well have been decided disapprobation, but 90
expressed in the language of a gentleman. And indeed it is
the very phrase that a courteous man would use in expressing
disappointment and dissatisfaction. There was the less occasion
for any violence of language, as by the letter to Kemble and the
refusal there expressed, the ill consequences of the unauthorized
order, would be avoided, and it would practically cease to have
any operation. And it may well be supposed that the intercourse
of many years had established such relations between the parties,
that rudeness or even strength of rebuke would have been quite
inappropriate. Under all the circumstances, it is submitted that 91
the language of Gen. Talcott was as decided disapprobation of
the order to Carmichael, as the occasion demanded.

Reliance was also evidently placed on the interviews of Capt.
Maynadier with Gen. Talcott, as evidence at least of knowledge,
if not of acquiescence or approval of the order to Carmichael.
The first of these was on the 11th of November (folio 194), when
Capt. M. informed Gen. T. of the report he had heard that Carmichael had obtained a big contract for shot from the ordnance
department, and had offered it for sale. The answer of Gen. T.
was precisely that which the facts justified; that he knew nothing 92
of such a contract, and that all that had been done in relation to
the purchase of shot, would be found on record in his letter of
November 6. An inattention to dates, may have misled the
judge advocate in respect to this conversation; it was on the 11th
of November (folio 194), and previous to the receipt of Mr. Kemble's letter of 17th November.

The other interview is related at folio 196 to 198, when Capt.
M. read to Gen. T. the letter of Mr. Anderson, given at length at
folio 210, and a copy of the order to Carmichael, and he made no
explanation. Why should he make any explanation? Capt. M. 93
knew the exact state of the case as well as Gen. T. The letter
to Kemble of November 21 (folio 101), had been written; Capt.
Stone had by order of Col. Huger, repudiated the transfer of the
order by Carmichael to Anderson (folio 109); and Gen. Talcott
had been informed of this act of Capt. Stone by Col. Huger (fol.
105, 106); and he had every reason to suppose that the order
was defunct, or at least could not be used to justify the delivery
of a large quantity of shot.

The testimoy of Major Mordecai (folio 250), seems also to have
been introduced for the same purpose. He sent guages to Anderson, in January, 1851, at the request of Col. Huger, and men- 94
tioned the fact to Gen. Talcott, presuming "there would be no
objection;" to which the General answered, "No, I suppose not."

Surely, this could not be deemed a sanction, in January, 1851,
of what had been expressly and directly repudiated by the letter
to Kemble of November 21, 1850, and by the official act of Capt,

Stone of November 26 (folio 109), and which he had disapproved
in his conversation with Huger. Major Mordecai, considered it
a matter of no importance, as the guages he supposed might be
95 wanted to make shot for experiments (folio 253).

There is still another piece of evidence of the same magnitude
and dignity. Morris Adler, a clerk in the bureau, of his own
accord, furnished to Carmichael on the 7th of November, (the
day after the letter to Huger,) the prices paid for shot (fol. 190),
and informed Gen. T. of his having done so, "who censured
him a good deal for having furnished the prices at all" (fol. 191).
What information did Adler give Gen. T. in reference to Carmichael's intention to make shot, if he could obtain an order, than
he already had, when he had delivered him his letter of November
96 6? The value of this evidence for any purpose, has escaped my
penetration.

We come now to consider a mass of evidence of the most extraordinary character. The prosecution offered in evidence letters which had passed between Col. Huger and Mr. Anderson
relating to the execution of the order given to Carmichael. The
accused objected to this evidence unless the letters were "in
pursuance of previous instructions from the accused or had been
subsequently ratified and adopted by him." (folio 111). The
court admitted it however, on the ground that "it was competent
for the prosecution to introduce testimony showing the carrying
97 into effect or execution of the order or contract" (folio 116).
That shot had been delivered by Anderson at Fort Monroe to a
large amount, was not questioned by any one. The correspondence was not necessary, or even a connecting link in the proof of
that fact. The witness Col. Huger, was on the stand to prove it
in ten words. The introduction of the correspondence was therefore an insidious and disingenuous attempt (I use these terms to
characterize a professional act) to smuggle testimony for another
purpose distinct from that which the court sanctioned, namely,
to cast upon Gen. Talcott the odium and suspicion which would
98 be excited by letters he had never seen, and which he never authorized or approved. Such a *naked* proposition would scarcely
be made in any court in Christendom. The judge advocate
therefore claimed the admission of these letters on the ground
that Col. Huger was *authorized* by Gen. Talcott to make the
contract with Carmichael (folio 114). And this is the only possible ground on which he could claim the admissibility of the letters in question. He did not pretend, and could not with any
consistency, that there was a conspiracy between Gen. Talcott
and Col. Huger to defraud the government, for then he would
99 have been bound to prosecute Col. Huger; and there is not a
scintilla of proof to support any such proposition.

It has already been shown, I trust to the satisfaction of every
reader, that the letter of November 6 did not authorize *the* order
of Huger to Carmichael. But assuming what has been thus dis-

proved, that there was presumptive evidence of such anthority to Huger, as would justify the admission of his declarations at all,
yet there was a palpable violation of plain and familiar princi- 100
ples of the law of evidence and of the dictates of common justice, in admitting the letters written at different times *after* the authority was executed and forming no part of the order supposed to have been authorized.

Col. Huger was himself an officer of the government and its agent, and he was in no sense the agent of Gen. Talcott. He was his subordinate officer and was bound to obey his orders, and he was justified in executing a mere authority relating to his duties, which did not amount to an order. The responsibility of
the superior was co-relative and extended no farther than the 101
authority he had given. So far then as Col. Huger was an agent of Gen. Talcott, it was special and limited. When he had given the order to Carmichael, he had done all that the letter of November 6 authorized. He was never authorized by Gen. T. to enter into explanations or negotiations either with Anderson, Kemble or any other person, or to hold any correspondence with them. And Gen. Talcott was no more responsible for what he said in his letters than the Secretary of War, whose agent Huger was, as far as he was under his control. No argument can be necessary to show that letters and declarations which were neither 102
authorized generally or specially by a party, nor ever came to his knowledge until his trial, can not be used as evidence against him. No example or parallel for such a proceeding can be found except in trials for treason in the worst times before such men as Jeffries; and these have been handed down not for imitation, but for execration. The whole of the mass of letters from folio 120 to 160, and those introduced by the Secretary at folio 351 to 374, under the pretext of being copies or originals of those he had sent to Gen. Talcott for explanation, were written long after the authority of November 6 had been executed by the order of Huger 103
to Carmichael and formed no part of that order. Whatever the contract between Huger and Carmichael was, it was finished, and no subsequent explanation of views and objects could affect it, nor could they derive any sanction from the original authority of November 6.

The declarations of an agent, says Ch. J. Dallas, "are only admitted as evidence when they form a part of the contract entered into by the agent on behalf of his principal; and in that *single* case they become admissible" (*Gow. N. P.*, 45).

There is another fatal objection to these letters, as declarations
of an agent or authorized person. The rule is inflexible that 104
such declarations must be part of the *res gesta* and must be made at the *very time* of the making of the contract; and those made at another time or on another occasion, are wholly inadmissible (*Story on Agency, sec.* 135, 136, 137; *Phillips on Evidence*, 73 to 77; *Starkie on Ev., part* 4, 42). From its very nature, Lord Ch.

Justice Tindal says, in 8 *Bingham,* 451, "such evidence ought always to be kept within the strictest limits to which the cases have confined it."

105 And this rule is founded in common justice and common sense. Who can be safe, if he is to be compromitted by one whom he had authorized to perform a single act, by the expressions of his apprehensions, or by his contrivances and devices to avoid an explosion long after the act of agency was completed? Col. Huger was seeking to extricate himself from difficulty. There is nothing in his letters indicating any knowledge by Gen. Talcott of their contents or of what was going on between Huger and Anderson. But there is such an air of mystification about them, such feeble explanations, such turnings and twistings, and above
106 all such maudlin apprehensions for Gen. Talcott, as were calculated to make a stronger impression on the court against the accused than any direct testimony could have effected, and stronger than all the other evidence in the case.

And yet no authority for these proceedings is traced to General Talcott, and no knowledge of them whatever or the least ground to suspect them. The only authentic knowledge he could have, was the receipt from Col. Huger of the *estimates* which in the letter of November 6, he was required to make, "to *meet* the deliveries as they occur" (folio 10). What officer would dream of deliveries
107 of articles being made, upon an engagement to pay for them on delivery, when he knew no funds had been provided for such payment? Huger says (folio 167) that "he never made any estimates ro report of what was doing." The very absence of these estimates was in itself evidence of the most satisfactory nature, that there could not be any shot or shells making or delivered under that letter. The very parties to the transaction, Huger and Anderson, on their oaths, and they are witnesses produced by the prosecution, expressly and unqualifiedly negative any such knowledge on the part of Gen. Talcott. At folio 165, Col. Huger says, "that he never had any communication, direct or indirect, official or
108 otherwise, with Gen. Talcott, touching the order to Carmichael, or the transfer to Anderson, after the refusal to recognize the transfer, (November 22; see Stone's letter, folio 106,) until ordered to report in April last." "None, whatever," says the witness. Even in his private examination before the Secretary (fol. 345), he had the resolution to say "he was *pretty certain*, Gen. Talcott was not informed that shot had been sent to Fort Monroe by Anderson, under the order given to Carmichael." And again in his testimony before the court, he says that he had never made known to the ordnance bureau or its chief, that Anderson was
109 employed in making shot and shells as set forth in the correspondence" (folio 174). Anderson, the other party to the correspondence and to the transactions in question, is equally explicit that "he never notified Gen. Talcott that he was executing the order of Col. Huger to Carmichael" (fol. 185, 186).

What friend of justice can repress his indignation at this attempt, alas! too successful, to sacrifice a brave old soldier by
means of acts of which he was kept in profound ignorance, and
of writings and letters between third parties that were equally 110
unknown to him until produced on the trial,—done and written
by persons for whose proceedings he was in no way responsible?

Space and time allow me only to point out the letter of Mr.
Kemble to Huger (folio 368), marked F, and to ask by what
strange process that letter became a part of the evidence? It is
explanatory of nothing, and certainly Mr. K. was not the agent
of Gen. Talcott.

Utterly rejecting, as the court should have done, the illegal and
grossly improper evidence of these letters, and purifying our
minds from their vile influences, let us revert to the other proof
to establish the great point in the case on which most of the 111
charges hinge and which the prosecution undertook to prove.
That point is the *knowledge* by Gen. Talcott, of the acts and proceedings of Anderson and Huger, in delivering and receiving the
shot and shells; for without such knowledge, there could be
neither acquiescence, approval or sanction. That other proof
consists of Gen. Talcott's approval of the answer by Huger to
Mr. Kemble; of his not more decidedly repudiating in his remarks
to Huger, his order to Carmichael; his interviews with Capt.
Maynadier; his knowledge that Major Mordecai had sent guages
to Anderson at the request of Huger, after the order to Car- 112
michael had been repudiated; and his censure of Adler for sending the prices of shot to Anderson. A very diligent scrutiny of
the whole record, has not enabled me to find a particle of testimony having the least relation to this question of knowledge, but
the parts now enumerated. These have been examined at large.
And may not the appeal be made to every unprepossessed mind,
whether more feeble grounds to support a charge of such gravity,
have been often presented in any court of justice? Weak and
inconclusive as they are, they are utterly destroyed by the testimony of the only persons besides Gen. Talcott who could speak 113
with certainty on the subject,—the two parties to the transactions,
Huger and Anderson, witnesses produced by the prosecution.
There is still another party to speak, whose testimony is also
produced by the prosecution,—Gen. Talcott himself, whose declarations in writing they have given in evidence for their own
purposes, and which they are therefore bound to acknowledge as
competent proof. At folio 385 Gen. Talcott says, "I knew not
that Mr. Anderson had gone on to fill Col. Huger's order. This
information was received by me subsequently, (to his report of
27th January,) and was stated in my report of 19th April." 114

After such an utter failure to establish the fact of knowledge by affirmative proof, and after such overwhelming testimony proving the negative, there is little occasion to call in the aid of presumptions against the probability—the possibility of a sane

man permitting such involvment of the department, and at the
same time denying its existence.

115 And yet, this fact of knowledge is all essential to this second
charge, as well as to subsequent ones, and with its fall, those
charges fall also.

Each one of the facts necessary to support this SECOND charge,
has failed in proof. 1st. It has not been proved that the Secretary of War made a decision amounting to orders and instructions
forbidding *any* contract with Carmichael; 2. Nor has it been
proved that the accused by his letter of November 6, intended to
authorize the order to Carmichael which was given by Huger;
3. Nor is it proved that the accused subsequently approved and
116 allowed that order to or contract with Carmichael.

The THIRD CHARGE against Gen. Talcott (fol. 18) is the most
general and indefinite known in any code, civil or military. In the
British articles of War from which ours were substantially copied,
this article, which is there numbered 26, describes the offence "of
behaving in a scandalous or infamous manner, such as is unbecoming the character of an officer and a gentleman." In our
article 83, the offence is described "as conduct unbecoming an
officer and a gentleman." The change probably does not materially
alter the offence, for it is difficult to conceive of conduct unbe-
117 coming an officer *and* a gentleman, which would not be scandalous
or infamous. The description given by Mr. Hough in his treatise
on Courts Martial, p. 496, is evidently equally applicable to the
English and the American article. "The misbehavior must arise
in some sort out of his office, so as to implicate him as *an officer*,
and affect incidentally only, his character as a gentleman. It
must be of that decidedly low, humiliating and debasing kind as
to lay prostrate the honor of the gentleman in the degradation of
the officer." The good sense of this description would commend
it to every discerning mind, without the sanction of any name.

118 The *first specification* under this charge (fol. 18), is that by his
letter to Huger of Nov. 6, *and* by his subsequent approval of the
contract made with Carmichael, Gen. Talcott caused a contract
to be made for a *large amount* of ordnance stores, which he knew
and had previously reported to the Secretary of War, were not
needed for public service.

The court having by their verdict acquitted Gen. Talcott of
that part of this charge which alleges that he "had previously
reported" were not needed for public service (fol. 462)), it is reduced to a charge of causing to be procured a large amount of
119 stores which he *knew* were not needed.

This specification is based on the assumption of the same facts
which constituted the main ground for the second charge, and
which have been so fully discussed; namely, the approval of
Huger's arrangement for procuring a *large amount* of shot and
shells. If there was no such approval, if the execution of the
orders to Carmichael was unknown to Gen. T., so that it could

not be approved by him, then of course this charge falls; and if it has not already been shown that there is a total failure of affirmtive proof to establish any such knowledge, and that the negative 120
has been conclusively proved by the prosecutor's witnesses, it would be idle to renew the effort here.

The charge is *not*, that by the letter of Nov. 6 alone, a greater amount of ordnance stores was ordered than he knew to be necessary, but that by that letter *and* the subsequent approval of the order to Carmichael and its execution by Anderson, a *large amount* of ordnance stores was contracted for which he knew were not needed for public service.

It is hardly necessary to quote the authority of Mr. Hough to such a principle of universal jurisprudence, but his language is so 121
apt, that I give it: "A court has in all cases to deal only with the criminal matter *charged* and no other." (p. 648)

The looseness of the charge deserves a moment's consideration. What sort of an offence is committed by a high military officer, who procures a larger amount of military stores, or of subsistence, or of transportation, than he knew the public service needed? Needed when? At the moment, or in future! To say nothing of commanding generals preparing for the field, how would such a charge affect quarter-masters and commissaries? What is needed, is matter of judgment, of discretion, and an un- 122
due excess can not be an offence, unless it be caused by some improper motive. No such motive or design is imputed in this specification, and it stands, therefore, a naked charge of procuring more ordnance stores than he knew were needed. How can a criminal offence be constructed from such materials? The court seem to have overlooked the *point* of the charge, "which he had previously reported to the secretary were not needed," and which if true, would render a subsequent order to the contrary disrespectful, disobedient and altogether disorderly and unbecoming. But having found that allegation false, they seem not to have 123
perceived that such finding carried with it the whole specification; and strangely found Gen. Talcott guilty of conduct unbecoming an officer and a gentleman: that his giving an order for a larger amount of stores than he knew the public service needed, was conduct of "that decidedly low, humiliating and debasing kind, as to lay prostrate the honor of the gentleman in the degradation of the officer." The finding of the court appears still more extraordinary, when we remember that the order which is thus stigmatized, was one for a limited quantity, to be furnished from time to time, as occasion required! For such, it has been shown, was 124
the only order for which Gen. Talcott was responsible.

There is an episode connected with this specification which should be mentioned before its consideration is dismissed.

The court found Gen. T. not guilty of having previously reported to the secretary as to the quantity of ordnance stores needed for the public service. The charges and specifications

purport to have been drawn up under the superintendence of the
Secretary of War (fol. 36). The Secretary, above all others,
125 knew whether such a report had or had not been previously made
to him. How then, came he to cause such an allegation to be inserted in the specification! Did his memory fail him in an act
of such momentous importance to a fellow citizen? Did his
imagination supply a fact of such significance? I am dealing with
the Secretary as a witness and a prosecutor, and he has no right
to interpose the shield of high office against the most rigid scrutiny to which any of his fellow citizens may be justly subjected.
I claim the right to impeach his testimony under the extraordinary
circumstances which will hereafter appear, by showing such a
126 wretched defect of memory and such an exuberance of imagination,
as led him to assert in a solemn charge, a fact which was wholly
unfounded; which he would not verify by his own oath, and which
a court of his own selection pronounced false.

The Second specification under this charge (fol. 19 to 22),
having been negatived by the finding of the court, folio 462, comment upon it is unnecessary except to exhibit the *animus* with
which it was made. Its point and essence is, that Gen. Talcott
by his letter of Nov. 6, and by his approval of Huger's arrangement with Carmichael, caused a contract to be made with a man
127 who *he knew* could not execute it, otherwise than by a sale of it
to some third person, and thereby knowingly and wilfully exposed
the government not only to the loss occasioned by an exorbitant
price having been allowed, but to the discredit and disgrace arising
from the sale of a public contract. Of course the evidence absolutely rebutted and destroyed the least pretext for such a charge.
But again, I ask, how came it among the specifications drawn up
under the superintendence of the Secretary of War? Look for a
moment at the excessive folly and unmitigated turpitude of the
conduct charged. No motive is assigned, no insinuation even
128 hazarded that Gen. Talcott was to derive or could possibly derive
any personal benefit from thus thrusting into the public shambles
for the benefit of speculators a contract made exorbitantly high
for the very purpose "wilfully"—of having it hawked about the
country.

What idea must a prosecutor have of the character, principle
or intelligence of the accused, who could prefer such a charge,
against him? To believe in the possibility of such egregious
wickedness and folly, one must have already brought his mind to
the conviction that the person capable of it, was a demon in hu-
129 man shape; and the presentation of this charge by the secretary,
thus opens a view of the state of his own mind, in relation to
Gen. Talcott, which has a very important bearing upon the
charges yet to be considered.

The remaining specifications of this charge, the 3d, 4th, 5th,
6th and 7th (folio 22 to 36), may be considered together. They
charge two distinct offences, varying only in the forms and times

of their alleged commission, and the proof in support of them is
the same. As these forms and modes are quite immaterial, if the
whole ground on which the assumed offences rest, utterly fails, 130
this examination will be devoted to the charges in all their breadth
and under any and all circnmstances.

The charges made by these specifications are, 1st, *concealment*
from the Secretary of War of the facts that Huger's order to
Carmichael had been transferred to Anderson. and that the latter
was engaged in executing it; 2d, wilfully *false representations*
by denials and otherwise to the Secretary, that any contract existed
with Carmichael under which Anderson or the Tredegar
works, or any other person was making and delivering shot and
shells at Fort Monroe. 131

It will be conceded by any one who takes the pains to read these voluminous specifications, that the above two points present their whole force and substance.

The evidence in support of them consists of Gen. Talcott's letter of January 27, 1851 (fol 29), and of the testimony of Mr. Conrad, the main witness for the prosecution.

The letter is again given at folio 288 in connexion with the call
of the Secretary which produced it. In that call the Secretary
requests to be informed *what contracts* have been made for shot
from the last appropriations; *how much* has been *furnished*, and 132
how much was yet to be furnished, and whether any further contracts
are contemplated (fol. 287). The answer is full and explicit;
"no contract has been made for shot by this department,
from the last appropriation, no shot have been furnished."

Had the answer stopped here, there might have been some
ground for alleging concealment of what had taken place. But
with the frankness of a soldier, Gen. Talcott adds, that supposing
the enquiry might have reference to the letter of November 6, he
subjoins a copy of the whole of it. And in order to satisfy the
Secretary that no deliveries had been made under it, that "no shot 133
had been furnished," he adds that the only estimate received from
Col Huger since the date of the letter of November 6, "*contains
nothing* for the purchase of shot." This refers to the instruction
at the close of the letter of November 6, "you will make the
necessary estimates of funds to *meet* the deliveries as they occur."
Referring the reader to the remarks already made in this Review
(folio 106, 107) upon this point of estimates, it is only necessary
now to observe that the omission by Col. Huger to furnish the estimates
which were indispensable to place him in funds to pay for
shot as it should be delivered, was in itself the most complete and 134
perfect proof that no shot had been delivered; because they were
to be paid for on delivery, and as they could not have been paid
for, from the want of any previous supply of funds, they could
not have been delivered.

Surely here was no concealment, no false representation, but a frank, manly and voluntary disclosure of all that was known on

the subject, pertinent to the enquiry, by the Chief of the Ordnance
Bureau. The Secretary viewed it in the same light. He says,
135 folio 291: "This answer being perfectly satisfactory, I ceased to
think on the subject," until his suspicions were subsequently
aroused. Why was this answer satisfactory? The Secretary had
previously been assured by Gen. Talcott, folio 270, that "no contract existed for shot, and that none was making at Richmond for
the Department." The repetition of that assurance in writing
could not add to its credibility. Is it not evident that it was the
frankness with which the letter of November 6 had been furnished—the manner in which abuse had been guarded against by
the instruction to forward estimates,—and the assurance that no
136 estimates had been received,—which produced this satisfaction?
And what has occurred to change that feeling? A suspicion indulged by the Secretary, that while Gen. T. was thus furnishing
him with satisfactory evidence that no shot had been delivered
at Fort Monroe, he yet knew perfectly well that Anderson was actually delivering large quantities under the order to Carmichael.
The Secretary was importuned by Mr. Thomas Green for a contract, whose success depended on showing that one had been made
with Carmichael and Anderson, and who seems to have been very
busy about the department in finding papers in the pigeon holes
137 where they belonged. The impressions which such a man would
be likely to make on the Secretary, are obvious enough.

The extraordinary statements of Col. Huger to the Secretary on
the secret and *ex parte* examination, which have been commented
on at folio 85 to 89, were calculated to strengthen and deepen
these impressions into conviction. It did not require a mind to
be already prepared to take fire on the application of such matches.
Still it so happens that the mind of the prosecuting witness was
already heated and in a condition to adopt the worst constructions
and the most degrading views of the conduct of Gen. Talcott. It
138 is a fact of such notoriety as to justify a reference to it on this
occasion, that an unfriendly state of feeling existed between the
Secretary and Gen. Talcott, arising out of an attempt of the former
to remove Col. Baker from the Watervliet arsenal, in which the
Secretary had been baffled by the sense of justice, firmness and
decision of the President. A result in which Gen. T. had had
some agency.

These circumstances combined to operate on the Secretary's
mind, and so to prepossess him against Gen. Talcott, that he was
morally incapable of a just and generous judgment in respect to
139 his conduct. The natural consequences developed themselves as
we have already partly seen. One of the most remarkable of
them was a private inquisition at his rooms, of Col. Huger, conducted doubtless with all the professional subtlety which shines
so conspicuously in the Secretary's testimony—but in the absence
of the party implicated, and unknown to him. The witness thus
interrogated was the man most interested to shift the responsi-

bility of his acts to the shoulders of another, and we have seen how he acquitted himself. The Secretary knows as well as any lawyer, how very difficult it is for a man to vary essentially from 140
his first statements of any transaction,—the natural sense of shame too often overcoming the love of truth. It was a great disadvantage therefore to Gen. Talcott, to procure from the one most acquainted with the subject, a preliminary *ex parte* statement in writing, to be filed among the archives of the war department, in perpetual memory of the supposed facts. Indeed, the whole transaction was more like the proceedings of the Star Chamber than those of any modern tribunals, and it is to be hoped for the credit of our government, that it will be suffered to remain unimitated and unrepeated, as it is unprecedented; a solitary ex- 141
ample of the effects of excited passion.

Instances of the effects of some similar cause have already been given, in the extraordinary insertion in the 1st specification of a fact which did not exist—a previous report respecting the quantity of ordinance stores needed for the public service; and in the savage character of the second specification already presented to the consideration of the reader. In his manner of giving his testimony, we have already seen the ridiculous position which the prosecuting witness chose to occupy in giving his reasons for making out a report and declaration from silence, and 142
from a possibility that he might think in a particular way. The same obliquity of judgment or of memory is evinced in another instance. At folio 414, 415, &c., it will be seen that the counsel for the defence endeavored to draw from the witness, Mr. Conrad, an answer calculated to show that in his conversations with Gen. Talcott about contracts for shot, he had referred to *large amounts*, and how adroitly the witness avoided giving such answer. When, however, the question was put whether Green's application was not for *a large quantity*, and whether his remarks to Gen. Talcott were not occasioned by that application, he answers, folio 143
415, "Mr. Green did not refer to any quantity. I presume he would have preferred a large contract to a small one; but he never intimated that he would not take a small one." The disingenuousness of the last clause of this answer is palpable. But there is a greater defect. By referring to Mr. Green's letter, folio 300, 301, it will be seen that he claims a promise to give a fair proportion of such shot as the department required; that such "fair proportion would be an amount equal to that which the Tredegar works (Anderson's,) have been authorized to exe- 144
cute." And he then says that the Tredegar works are "now engaged in executing *a large amount* of work for the delivery of shot and shells." At folio 302, he says, "If you will direct an order to be given to Mr. Deane for a like amount of shot and shell as that which is authorized by the order under which Mr. Anderson is working, Mr. Deane will be satisfied." What must be the condition of that memory which could describe such an

application as not referring to any quantity! and what the state
145 of that mind which in answering an enquiry as to the contents
of an application, should proceed to state what it did *not* intimate. Indeed, much of the testimony of this witness is of the same argumentative character, full of inferences and deductions, and flanked by suggestions and impertinent observations to give a complexion to the case in harmony with his own jaundiced view of it.

It must not be supposed that these remarks are made respecting the main witness for the prosecution, wantonly or for the purpose of indulging any feeling of animosity, by a friend of Gen.
146 Talcott. They are made reluctantly, but under an imperious
conviction that they are essential to the formation of a just opinion of the weight which his testimony was entitled to have in the decision of the court. He instituted the prosecution, he appeared voluntarily as a witness in its support, and thereby cast off any and all the privileges of office, if any there be in such circumstances, and placed himself in the position which any respectable private citizens of the United States must occupy when testifying in a court of justice. His reputation was not fairer before this trial than that of Gen. Talcott. He has had no hesitation or
147 scruple in assailing that of an old soldier, and has no right to
complain of any fair or just comments on the exhibition he has made of himself, when such comments are necessary to the vindication of his victim. The forbearance which the generosity or the prudence of the counsel for the defence exhibited on the trial towards this witness, has been turned into a weapon against the accused, and a mass of suspicions, surmises, inferences, and incoherent, illegal and impertinent testimony has been allowed to sink into the minds of honest men as matter of great weight and importance, merely because it was not dissected and exposed.
148 Let it be understood, then, that in thus exhibiting the character
of Mr. Conrad's testimony, no reference is made to the man as an individual or an officer, but solely to the prosecutor and the witness.

These observations seemed necessary previous to an examination of the residue of testimony adduced to support the specifications of this 3d charge. That evidence consists wholly of conversations between the witness, Mr. Conrad, and the accused, Gen. Talcott, at which no other person was present, or to which no other person has testified. And they were had with a
149 person known to his friends, although perhaps not to Mr. Conrad,
to have had for some years an increasing difficulty in hearing. Not content with relating conversations, the witness was indulged in giving his impressions, his inferences from what was said and done, or omitted to be said, and his reasonings in support of such inferences. Some familiarity with actual trials, and with the reports of the most important that have ever occurred in this country or in England, enables the writer to challenge the production of one in which such a latitude, apparently without bound or limit, was

given to the garrulity of a witness. Rarely is a question directly
answered, but generally indefinitely and argumentatively. 150

To establish the justice of these remarks concerning the general character of Mr. Conrad's testimony, by quoting the particular passages, would be a repetition of whole pages of the record, and would expand this review beyond endurance. The writer can therefore do no more than request the reader to peruse the testimony from folio 62 to 86, and from 414 to 431.

The witness was in the position which all prosecuting witnesses occupy. His own reputation was at stake. The honorable acquittal of Gen. Talcott, necessarily involved the scandal of
having made accusations equally false and unjust, and of having 151
subjected an innocent man to the ignominy of such atrocious
charges. Indeed, higher responsibilities than usual attached to
the result; a hostile political majority in both houses of Congress,
might make it the occasion of such enquiries and proceedings as
would render the tenure of the office of Secretary of War quite
insecure.

Under all these circumstances, with the feelings, prejudices,
motives and consequences which have been described, this witness relates the conversations which he alleges took place be- 152
tween him and Gen. Talcott, on four or five different occasions,
at which no other person was present, and of course when there
could be no other witness to explain or contradict his testimony.

These conversations occurred before the interview with Mr. Anderson, which was about the 13th of April, folio 305.

Not a single fact or circumstance of any kind is brought forward to corroborate the statements of these conversations.

What has been said in reference to the testimony of Mr.
Conrad, has been with the view of presenting the question distinctly to every intelligent and unbiassed reader, whether it 153
should not be received with great allowances for mistakes and
errors arising from a defective memory, a lively imagination,
horrible prejudices, feelings of resentment, vindictiveness of
purpose, and apprehension of disgrace?

And now against such testimony is opposed that bulwark of the innocent, an untarnished reputation earned by nearly forty years of public service; the supreme folly of the imputed offences, and the absence of all motive for committing them. Upon this issue let every impartial man judge as he would be judged.

But there is a view of these specifications, still more conclu- 154
sive. Assuming that all the representations stated by Mr. Conrad
to have been made to him by Gen. Talcott were actually made,
precisely as he relates them, and that nothing has been forgotten
or omitted, still the facts of wilful concealment and intentional
falsehood are not established until something further is proved by
the most satisfactory evidence. There can be no concealment of
that which is not known; there can be no intentional falsehood
in representing facts according to the knowledge and honest be-

lief of the party. Hence, when the prosecution charges a *wilful*
155 concealment of the fact that Anderson was fabricating shot under
a transfer of the order to Carmichael, and had actually delivered
considerable quantities, they are bound to prove clearly that such
fact was known to the accused. And when it charges *intentional*
falsehood in repsesenting that no shot were making under that
order, and that none had been delivered, it must prove that
the accused knew the contrary. The burthen of this proof is
on the prosecution. In any case such knowledge should be
satisfactorily established; in the present case, the presumptions already presented in this review, are so strong against
156 the possibility of the accused having possessed the knowledge
imputed to him, that it should be established by such irrefragable
and conclusive testimony as will not admit of a reasonable doubt.

It were worse than useless to repeat what has already been
said in considering the second charge, upon this great and turning point in the case. So far from the prosecution having exhibited any evidence that Gen. Talcott knew or could have known
that Anderson was fabricating shot and delivering them, under
the order to Carmichael, the testimony of the witnesses produced
by the judge advocate is overwhelming that Gen. T. was kept in
157 profound ignorance of Anderson's proceedings, that he was misled by the omission of Col. Huger to forward estimates, and that
he had every reason to believe that the repudiation of Carmichael's attempted transfer to Kemble and to Anderson, had
effectually and finally baffled that gentleman's schemes.

And thus the fabric raised by these specifications, is dissolved, and leaves not a rack behind.

There was no concealment of any fact which Gen. T. was required to state, and there was no wilful falsehood in misrepresenting
facts different from his knowledge and understanding of them.
158 But there was a withholding of information calculated seriously
to implicate Col. Huger. At folio 303 the question is put
whether Gen. T. in his interview of 27th January, told the Secretary *how* Col. Huger had construed the letter of November 6,
and what he had done under it? and at folio 404 the question
is put more generally. To both, the witness answers in effect
that he never had. As the writer is not the partisan of Gen.
Talcott or of any other man, and has no desire to screen him
from censure when justly due, he admits that in his view Gen.
Talcott committed an error in this particular, which has given
159 the prosecution an advantage of which they have skillfully availed
themselves, to excite prejudice. Let us ascertain precisely the
nature, extent and criminality of this error.

There was no enquiry made by the Secretary to which an answer in exact accordance with the truth might not be given, without stating *how* Huger had construed the letter of Nov. 6, or what *had been done* under it. The enquiry invariably was, whether any contract *existed* for shot, and whether any *was*

making at Richmond (the Tredegar works) for the department,
folios 269, 270. Whether there were any existing contracts?
folio 273. What contracts have been made for shot from the last 160
appropriations; how much *has been furnished*, and how much yet
to be furnished? folio 287, &c. So at folio 303, that there was no
truth in the statement contained in Green's letter, of shot being
made at Richmond and delivered at Fort Monroe. Indeed, it is
only necessary to refer to the specifications under the third charge
(folios 22 to 36) relating to this point, and to ask the reader to peruse them to show that they charge the answers to have been given
to enquiries relating exclusively to an *existing* contract and actual
deliveries under it. Now it has been shown that as far as the
knowledge or information of Gen, Talcott extended, there was no 161
existing contract and no deliveries under it; and in saying so he
declared the exact truth, and fully and directly met the enquiries.

To this general remark respecting the enquiries made and the
answers given, there is an exception, which demands notice. At
folios 291 to 293, Mr. Conrad states as a witness, that "a short
time after" the letter of 27th January, he had an interview
with Gen. Talcott, and asked him whether the letter or order of
November 6 might not be construed to authorize the making of
shot, and what he meant by it? The answer was substantially
that the object of his letter was to authorize the purchase of shot 162
and shells as they were needed; and that they could only be
wanted for artillery practice and experiments; and then this remarkable sentence occurs: "that it was possible Col Huger might
have ordered something of this kind, but that it must of course
be a very inconsiderable quantity." Here was apparently a
concealment of the truth. It was not only possible, but at this
time Gen. T. had been fully apprised by the letter of Kemble, the
interviews with Col Huger, and in various other ways, that Col.
Huger had given an order for a large quantity of shot, which Carmichael had endeavored to sell. According to this statement of 163
the Secretary, here was a misrepresentation or a concealment of
transactions, the written evidence of which was on the files of the
war department, and which were known to various persons. Is
it credible, on its face, that such a gross and foolish falsehood
should have been uttered under such circumstances? It is submitted that enough has been shown in the course of this review
to justify if not to require great caution in receiving the testimony
of Mr. Conrad, to excite doubt of the accuracy of his memory, and
above all, doubt of his mind being in that calm, unprejudiced and
impartial condition, which would prevent any coloring or exaggera- 164
tion. In regard to this particular testimony as to the above extraordinary language imputed to Gen. Talcott, the doubt is greatly
strengthened by a singular fact. On the 1st of May 1851, the
Secretary wrote a letter to Gen. Talcott (folios 323 to 337), giving
a full and quite minute detail of the occurrences in relation to
the contract or order for shot, in which the conversations with

Gen. Talcott are particularly detailed. This was written for the purpose of eliciting explanations (fol. 337). At folio 325 he refers
165 to the letter of January 27, 1851, and the copy attached to it of Gen. Talcott's letter to Huger of November 6, and says: "In a conversation with you on the subject of this letter, you stated its object was to enable the commander of the arsenal at Fort Monroe to purchase shot and shells in small quantities as were required from time to time for experiments and artillery practice." And this is all he says respecting that conversation. By recurring to folio 291, it will be seen that this is the same conversation there testified to by the Secretary.

The reader will observe that in the written statement of
166 May 1, no mention whatever is made of the extraordinary remark testified to at folio 293, that it was *possible* Col. Huger might have ordered a few shot—a very inconsiderable quantity. I dwell not on the rule that when a witness gives different relations of the same transaction his testimony is invalidated, because ordinary rules seem not to be regarded as applicable to a witness of such dignity. But, I ask, which statement is the most to be depended upon—the deliberate and evidently cautious summing up of all the facts and circumstances, in the letter of May 1, or the verbal testimony of the substance of a conversation without
167 giving the words used? The letter was written to obtain explanations; what was there in the whole case that so much required explanation, as such a palpable evasion, concealment and suppression as would have been exhibited if such a remark had actually been made by Gen. Talcott? In all the other instances he was not required to state how Huger had construed the order, &c., but in this, Gen. T. was called upon, according to the Secretary's recollection, to answer that very point, and the Secretary testifies, answered it by a statement that conveyed a false impression to his mind. One would suppose such a statement, so palpably dis-
168 ingenuous and evasive, would have been uppermost in his mind, and would have been among the very first of the matters requiring explanation. And yet it is not adverted to in the slightest manner, nor is any explanation of it sought in the letter. The reader must determine under the circumstances whether the witness's memory was not as much at fault in stating the remark about the possibility of Huger's ordering only a few shot, as it was when he inserted in the second charge a report that was never made, or when he gave the substance of Mr. Green's application for a contract,

169 It is enough for the purpose of this review to remark that it would be utterly unsafe to convict any man of any serious charge, upon such testimony.

As already shown, in all the other conversations and communications, the enquiries related to an *existing* contract transferred to Anderson, under which he was *at the time* delivering shot and shell, These enquiries were answered truly according to the

then knowledge of the accused. But in the opinion of the writer, Gen. Talcott on those occasions, in justice to himself, if not in candor to the Secretary, should have gone further and stated fully, 170
precisely what had occurred and how the schemes of Carmichael had been baffled.

In his letter of explanation to the Secretary, folio 383, he furnishes a clue to his motives and feelings. He says: "In some stage of this matter, I may have displayed too much tenderness for a brother officer; in such a case, I would rather suffer wrong than do wrong." Col. Huger had seriously compromitted himself by a palpable departure from his instructions; but the evil had been remedied and all mischief prevented, as Gen. Talcott supposed, by the letter of Col. Huger to Kemble, and by the com- 171
munication of Capt. Stone to Anderson. The public interest did not require the sacrifice of one whom he had regarded as a worthy officer, for what might well be considered a mistake of judgment. The severe censure passed upon Col. Huger in the order of the President, is the best evidence of the correctness of Gen. Talcott's apprehensions. A full statement of all that had occurred would completely exonerate him, but it would or might ruin his friend. He preferred to stand the chance of censure for silence, when no public good required him to become an informer. And for this act of disinterestedness and generosity, which a selfish man could not have performed, he was arraigned for conduct unbecoming an 172
officer and a gentleman!, of conduct, "of that decidedly low, humiliating and debasing kind, as to prostrate the honor of the gentleman in the degradation of the officer." To every man of honor in the nation, I appeal, whether a course of conduct the direct opposite of that which he pursued—whether a full disclosure of the rashness and imprudence of Col. Huger at once, and a public disavowal of his proceedings, when they no longer threatened the public interests, and when the only effect would have been to excuse and perhaps glorify himself at the expense of another—whether such a course would not have better entitled him to the 173
infamy of having prostrated the honor of the gentleman in the degradation of the officer?

This review draws to a close. There are four distinct charges upon which Gen Talcott has been found guilty:

I. Violation of the 132d article of the regulations of the ordnance department. It is believed that it has been shown,

1. That the charge imputes no offence.
2. That the regulation does not apply to the Chief of the Bureau.
3. That it does not apply to an open purchase. 174
4. The order complained of was not without the sanction of the Secretary of War, but pursuant to his decision in approving the estimates.
5. The Secretary recognized and acknowledged the authority.

II, Willful disobedience of orders and instructions; an examination of the case shows,

175 1. An utter failure of the testimony to prove any decision of the Secretary that no contract or order whatever for shot should be given to Carmichael; and indeed that the Secretary refused to testify positively to his having given any such instructions.

2. That the Secretary himself, at the time, did not believe there had been a violation of the regulation in question, but of another, that he supposed had been made prior to the acts complained of.

3. The letter of November 6, did not authorize the purchase of a large quantity of shot, as alleged; and the Secretary did not so
176 understand it when he expressed himself satisfied with it.

4. The evidence wholly fails to establish affirmatively any knowledge by Gen. Talcott of Anderson's proceedings in fabricating shot and delivering them at Fort Monroe, under the order to Carmichael; and on the contrary the proof is positive and conclusive, from the prosecutor's witnesses that he was kept in profound ignorance of those proceedings, and was induced by Col. Huger to believe that no shot had been delivered or were in the course of delivery.. That illegal and incompetent testimony was admitted to support this charge in violation of the first principles of justice
177 and of law.

III. The first specification of the third charge, that Gen. Talcott had authorized the purchase of a large quantity of ordnance stores which he knew were not needed for the public service, to which it was reduced by the finding of the court,

In respect to this charge, it is maintained,

1. That it can not be an offence "unbecoming an officer and a gentleman," to purchase a greater quantity of military stores than he knew were needed; if an offence at all, it is one of a totally different description.

178 2. That from the nature of the case, it is impossible to say what an officer knew at any given time would or would not be needed in future.

3, That he did not authorize the purchase of ordnance stores to an amount beyond what he deemed necessary, but authorized their purchase "to a limited extent," and "from time to time," as occasion required; and always held in his own hands the means of restraining undue purchases.

IV. The charge of fraudulent concealment and willful falsehood in respect to the execution by Anderson of the order of Huger to
179 Carmichael. These charges have been met,

1. By showing that the evidence adduced to support them consists of a letter which gave the Secretary information of the letter of November 6, and the state of things as Gen. Talcott honestly believed them to exist; and of private conversations between the accusing witness and the defendant, which no other witness could be called to explain or contradict.

2. That the circumstances under which the testimony of the
only witness on the subject, was given, his state of mind, his prejudices, his motives, his mistakes and contradictions, so impair its 180
strength and entire credibility; that without imputing any design
to violate the truth, no impartial and intelligent tribunal could
found a verdict upon it alone, without corroborating evidence, and
that none such has been produced.

3. That there could be no concealment of what was unknown,
and that there could be no intentional falsehood in representing facts according to the knowledge and honest belief of the party;
and that the proof is absolutely overwhelming that Gen. Talcott
did not know and was kept in ignorance of the facts he is charged
with having concealed and misrepresented. 181

V. It has been admitted that Gen. Talcott committed an error of judgment in his desire to save his friend, by omitting to inform the Secretary of Huger's order to Carmichael, of its attempted transfer to Kemble and Anderson, and of the whole having been arrested and defeated. But it is contended that so far from this having been unbecoming an officer *and* a gentleman, it was a noble exhibition of the honorable feelings of a generous superior officer, and of a disinterested, self-sacrificing gentleman.

There is every reason for believing that this error, combined
with the illegal testimony that was introduced, the confused man- 182
ner in which the whole evidence was presented, and the impertinent surmises, inferences, reasonings and suspicions of the principal witness, operated upon the minds of the members of the
court, so as to induce them hastily—without due consideration,
to pronounce their verdict of guilty, and to award the sentence
of dismissal. In this case, as in that of Admiral Byng, the court
"committed a fatal error, and confounded the two ideas, neglect
of duty, and error of judgment."

That even under their view of the case, the court should have
awarded the extreme sentence of dismissal from the service, has 183
excited and continues to excite astonishment. It has been said
that under the 83d article of war, an officer convicted of conduct
unbecoming an officer and a gentleman, *must* be dismissed the service, and that the court had no discretion. If this opinion did
indeed cause the sentence, then is it another instance of lament-
able mistake of the law and practice of courts martial. The
analagous British article 26, contains the same declaration as
ours, "shall be discharged from the service." And yet, Mr.
Hough's treatises on Courts Martial and Military Courts, contain
numerous cases where Courts Martial have imposed punishments 184
of a less degree, after conviction upon charges under their 26th
article, which have been approved by the highest authorities in
the English service. Hough, 505 to 512. Hough, Military Courts,
passim.

The 2d of the British articles of war gives general authority to courts martial to punish "for conduct to the prejudice of good order and military discipline," in their discretion. And under

this authority they refrain, where the circumstances justify it,
185 from awarding the sentence of dismissal or discharge, although the conviction would warrant such a sentence, and impose a lighter punishment.

Our article 99 contains the same provision as the British 2d article, and gives power to punish "all crimes not capital and all disorders and neglects which officers and soldiers may be guilty of, to the prejudice of good order and military discipline, though not mentioned in the foregoing articles of war, according to the nature and degree of the offence, at their discretion"

It is a well settled principle, applicable to courts martial and
186 all other courts, that although all the facts stated in the charge be proved, the jury or court acting in its place, must judge for itself of the *intent* of the accused, and the extent of his criminality. Hough, 499.

Indeed this is the very province of a jury, and the main purpose for which it is empannelled. Every one knows the daily practice to find all the facts stated in an indictment for murder and yet to render a verdict for manslaughter; or upon a charge of robbery to find it larceny or simple assault. A court martial is in the place of a jury and exercises all its functions. Although
187 it may find all the facts to be true which are stated in a specification under a charge of conduct unbecoming an officer and a gentleman, yet, if in their judgment the intent or motives of the accused and the circumstances of the case, do not establish that degree of criminality which is so degrading and derogatory as to require dismissal, it is as much their duty to render a verdict for an offence of an inferior degree, as it is of a jury in a criminal case. Hence it is, that courts martial in England, and it is presumed in this country, while they may find the facts which the prosecutor charges and which he claims constitute one grade of
188 offence, yet are they not bound by his classification, but may declare an offence the punishment of which may be apportioned in their discretion to the true circumstances of the case.

If then, the court believed that Gen. Talcott's conduct had in any instance been "to the prejudice of good order and military discipline"—terms sufficient to cover any irregularity or impropriety,—then by the 99th article and by military usage and universal precedent in civil cases, it possessed the discretion to award the sentence according to that article. And I fearlessly put the question to every honorable and impartial mind, whether
189 any error, irregularity or impropriety he may have committed in not sacrificing his friend and subordinate officer, should not have been classed under the offence of conduct "to the prejudice of good order and military discipline, rather than that of "conduct unbecoming an officer and gentleman"? And if the court acted under the fatal mistake that this was beyond their power, ought there not to be some remedy to correct the error and avert its terrible consequences?

But if the writer has succeeded in establishing, as he trusts
and believes he has, that by no just construction of our 83d arti- 190
cle could any act of Gen. Talcott's be deemed conduct unbecoming an officer and gentleman—" so decidedly low, humiliating and
debasing as to lay prostrate the honor of the gentleman in the
degradation of the office," then the sentence of the court, under
this mistaken view of the evidence and the law, shocks the moral
sense.

If there be any mode known to our constitutional system of
government, by which a verdict founded on illegal testimony and
wholly unsupported by the evidence may be examined, and a
harsh and unjust sentence may be reversed; and it is believed 191
there are such modes, then it is confidently submitted, the present
is a case in which such a remedy should be applied. While in
theory a review is provided by requiring the approval of the sentence by the President, yet practically it can be of little avail.
Military discipline requires a promptness of decision, quite unfavorable to the careful and deliberate examination of voluminous
testimony, presented in the most disorderly and confused manner,
and involving the discussion of critical questions of evidence. In
all other proceedings, civil or criminal, there is always ample
time allowed for men prepared by professional training, to ana- 192
lyze the record of the case, compare the different parts, discover
the incongruities and contradictions, dispel illusions, reduce the
facts to system and point out the just inferences from them, and
above all, to investigate the legal questions involved, and present
those views of the case which study and reflection enable
them to show are the true and just conclusions to be drawn from
it. In this case, it appears from the record that the court
finished its labors and pronounced its decision on the same day,
after an elaborate defence was read by the counsel for the
accused (folio 461). As the court could not sit after three o'clock 193
in the afternoon, how brief a space did it allow itself for the
examination of 256 folio pages of manuscript and giving to it the
consideration which the defence of the accused obviously required.
The approbation of the President is dated on the next day, and the
court was dissolved at 10 o'clock in the morning of that day. It
is impossible that in the interval between the transmission of the
record to the President after 3 o'clock P. M. of the 7th of July,
and 10 o'clock A. M. of the 8th, that such consideration could
have been given to such voluminous testimony presented as this
was, as is given by courts of appeal in civil cases. 194

The writer imputes no blame to the President. He under-
stands very well the position in which that excellent chief magis-
trate was placed. The idea of any legal question existing in the
case, had not been presented. It appeared to be wholly a question
of evidence, on which eleven of the most distinguished officers of
the army had pronounced their verdict. It related to military
matters with which they were supposed to be most familiar; and

having a just confidence in their integrity and impartiality, he
195 could not undertake to reverse their finding unless he found such
gross and palpable mistakes as would ordinarily warrant a court
in setting aside the verdict of a jury. And how, without the aid
of counsel for the defence to point out such mistakes, and which
neither law nor usage allowed,—how could they be discovered in
such a heterogeneous mass?

A safeguard against the errors of military courts interposed
by the British laws, does not exist in our system. With that
watchful care of the personal security of its subjects which dis-
tinguishes the British constitution, its laws provide an appeal to
196 the civil courts from any decision of a court martial, even after it
has been approved by the King; and the superior courts of the
kingdom examine the proceedings to ascertain whether there has
been any irregularity, any illegal evidence, or any finding against
the decided preponderance of testimony. in the same manner and
with the same authority to reverse, correct and modify, as in civil
cases. Tytler, 167, 168. Opinions of Attorney General, p. 173.

Under such circumstances, it would be a reproach to the justice of our country, if there were not some mode by which the proceedings of the court could be re-examined; and if found justified by the law and the evidence, affirmed and sustained; but if found erroneous, contrary to law and utterly unsupported by evidence, corrected, and justice vindicated. The whole matter is within the control of an enlightened and honest President whose pride of opinion will never constrain him to maintain wrong, and of an honorable, learned and independent Senate, whose character is a pledge to the world that they will dispense impartial justice to all.

REGULARITY OF THE CONSTITUTION OF THE COURT.

I have reserved for a separate examination, a question of con- 197
siderable importance which arises upon the face of this record
respecting the organization of the court martial. The 64th of the
articles of war provides that "General courts martial may consist of any number of officers from five to thirteen inclusively;
but they shall not consist of less than thirteen, where that number can be convened without manifest injury to the service."

This provision was the subject of judicial construction by the
Supreme Court of the state of New-York, in 1821, reported in
19th Johns. Rep., p. 7 to 38. Mills vs. Martin. Platt, J., in
delivering the judgment of the court, p. 29, says: "I admit that the 198
officer instituting the court martial is to judge and decide on the
point of "manifest injury to the service." But I contend that he
is bound to *adjudicate* and express his opinion to that effect
whenever he directs a General Court Martial to consist of less
than thirteen members, and the fact of manifest injury to the
service ought to have been averred, in order to show jurisdiction
in six members only." Spencer, Ch. J. concurred in the judgment of the court upon the ground that it was not stated in the
proceedings who, or by what authority the court martial was
convened. "The court being called into existence for a special 199
and limited purpose, existing only temporarily, and *pro hac vice*,
it must be organized agreeably to law, and this must be shown
definitely and distinctly, for it is a traversable fact."

A similar case, Martin vs. Mott, came before the Supreme
Court of the United States, and is reported in 12 Wheaton's Reports, 19 to 39. A very material difference however, existed in
the pleadings. In the New York case there was no averment
whatever respecting the manifest injury to the service by con-
vening a less number than thirteen, or that any decision on the
subject had been made. But in the case in Wheaton it was ex- 200
pressly averred, p. 21, that it had been "considered and adjudged
by the said Morgan Lewis, (who had ordered the court,) that a
greater number of officers than those detailed on the said court
martial, could not be spared from the service of the United States
without manifest injury to the said service." Story, J., giving
the opinion of the court, when adverting to the objection against
the number of the court martial, says: "Supposing these clauses
applicable to the court martial in question, it is very clear that
the act is merely directory to the officer appointing the court, and
that his decision as to the number which can be convened without manifest injury to the service, being in a matter submitted to 201
his discretion, must be conclusive." In an opinion given by
Attorney General Taney (vol. 1 Opinions of Attorney General,
p. 889,) he quotes this language of Justice Story, and confirms
the conclusion that there must be *a decision* of the fact that a
greater number can not be convened without manifest injury to

the service, *by the officer ordering the court.* He considers the
202 fact, that the order directed the court to consist of six members, as in itself a decision that no more could be spared without injury to the service.

It is submitted that there was no such adjudication or decision, in the case of Gen. Talcott. The order, folio 1, directs a general court martial to consist of *thirteen* members, to assemble, &c., for the trial, and gives their names. So far, here is a decision that the whole number of thirteen *may be* convened without manifest injury to the service.

The order then proceeds, folio 3; "Should any of the officers
203 named in the detail be prevented from attending at the time and place specified, the court will nevertheless proceed to and continue the business before it, provided the number of members present be not less than the minimum prescribed by law."

Here is no appearance of any adjudication that the whole number could not be convened without manifest injury to the public service. Upon the principles stated, the President could not have delegated to the members who should meet, or to any other persons or officers, the authority to decide whether the public service would be injured by the attendance of the full number.
204 But he did not attempt to give them any such authority. He says nothing about injury to the service, but leaves the number of the members of the court to depend entirely on the accident whether "any of the officers *named in the detail*" should be prevented from attending. A majority of those officers might be thus *prevented*, and yet there may have been a sufficient number out of the large number of the officers of the army, who could have been assembled without injury to the service. The prevention by accident or otherwise of the attendance of *these particular officers named,* does not imply or authorize the implication
205 that there was not an abundance of other officers who could be spared for the duty.

If, on the principle of construing the whole of an instrument together, the last clause is to be considered as qualifying the first clause, and the order itself therefore indefinite as to the number of the members, then it prescribed no number, but left it to chance and accident.

But if the first part of the order directing the court to "consist of thirteen members" is to be deemed a *decision* upon the principles before stated and relied on by Attorney General Taney, that
206 that number may be spared, then it stands until revoked. Surely there is nothing in the last clause inconsistent with the *fact* thus decided. It is a dispensing clause, reducing the number required by law, upon grounds and for reasons not recognized by law as sufficient for that purpose.

The British articles of War prescribe simply, the least number of which a court martial shall consist. It is the practice there to detail this minimum number and then add supernumeraries; so that if any of the first named be absent, the legal number may be supplied. See Hough and Tytler on Courts Martial.

Our article differs from the British only in giving the maximum 207
thirteen, but it is precisely like it in prescribing the minimum, that it must consist of five members at least: hence our practice has been like that of the British. The order designates the number of which the court martial *shall* consist, it then details the officers; and it then adds supernumeraries to take the place of any who may be absent, and thus complete the number decided upon to compose the court. See opinions of Attorney General, vol. 1, p. 522. The error in the order in this case, was either 1st, in fixing on the largest number, 13, and omitting to name supernumeraries to complete it; or, 2d, in not fixing on 11, 10, 9, or 208
some other definite number.

When it was found that the whole number had not assembled, the remaining members were bound to wait until all reasonable prospect of the attendance of those who were absent, had failed, and report the facts to the Adjutant General for such further order as the President might direct. Nothing of the kind was done. After waiting one day and part of another for Gen, Clark, the court organized at once. The precipitancy of the step was shown by the fact that on the very next day, Wednesday the 25th of June, Gen. Clark appeared in the court, reported himself to the 209
President, and no notice whatever was taken of him!

The fact of his appearance does not appear on the record, but the newspaper reports of the day stated it, and there is an affidavit in the possession of Gen. Talcott, establishing it.

But the fact does appear distinctly, that the court organized (fol. 6) and proceeded with the trial (fol. 75), in the absence of Gen. Clark; with but 12 members a portion of the time, and with 11 after the first five days, Gen. Walbeck, an officer nearly 90 years old, being obliged to leave the court from sickness (fol. 224).

This question of the number of members of which a court shall 210
consist, goes to its jurisdiction. This is admitted in the cases cited from Johnson's reports and Wheaton's reports, and in the opinion of Attorney General WIRT, p. 522, Opinions of Attorney General. And when J. Story in the case in Wheaton, speaks of the article being *directory* to the officers appointing the court, he means that it was discretionary; for he says so afterwards, and then adds that the exercise of the discretion, by a *decision* must be conclusive.

The court stand in the place of a jury, which must by the common law consist of 12, and can be neither more nor less. Bacon 211
Ab. Juries, A. A trial by a less number is a mistrial, absolutely void; and even a custom to try by six jurors, and to which neither party objected at the time, was held void and the verdict set aside. *Cro. Charles*, 259. Consent even, much less silence, will not give jurisdiction or cure the want of it. And whenever the want of jurisdiction appears, the judgment will be void. 1 Hill (N. Y.) Reports, 130, 343.

Surely the considerations which induced two Attorneys General
of the U. States to advise the setting aside the finding of a Court
212 martial because the Judge Advocate was not sworn (Opinions of
Att'y Gen. p. 1229 and 1330), sink into insignificance when compared with those applicable to the present question.

In prescribing the number 13, when that number could be assembled without injury—without *manifest* injury, Congress intended to throw a shield around the accused analagous to that of
trial by jury in criminal cases. Public considerations as well as
private rights, demand such a provision. If the law can be dis-
pensed with, arbitrarily or without the existence of the only cause
specified, the dearest interests, the honor, the life of the soldier
213 may be placed at the mercy of a few men selected by the accuser.
Every one knows the futility of the right of challenge in most
cases. There may be feelings, prejudices, subserviency to power,
dread of displeasing superiors, which can not be reached by a
challenge. The security of the accused is guarded by multiply-
ing the number of his triers, because the chances of impartiality
are increased by the greater difficulty of corrupting or influencing
a large number.

How can this inestimable right be made to depend upon the
accident of members being *prevented* from attending! What
214 is meant by beiug prevented? The convenience of an officer in
traveling; his wish to enjoy the comforts of a city through which
he may be passing, and even his unwillingness to sit on a case of
great responsibility—or in one between the cabinet minister
having charge of the army and an humble officer;—these and a
hundred other similar canses may *prevent* his attendance. The
accused has no means of compelling such attendance, while the
accuser has.

In every view, therefore, in which this question can be considered, it is respectfully submitted, that a great and fundamental
215 irregularity has occurred in the organization of the court martial,—that the court did not consist of the number required by
law; that the only exception allowed has not been established in
the only way in which it could be done; that the order was irre.
gular in leaving the number to accident, whim or caprice; that
the objection affects the jurisdiction of the court and renders its
verdict and its judgment void: and that the objection has not
been and can not be waived.

A precedent for the proper mode of remedying the consequences
of such an illegal and void sentence, is furnished in the opinion
216 of Attorney General Berrien, in 1831, in the case of John H.
Clark (Opinions of Atty Gen. 808, 809). There was an irregularity which vitiated the proceedings of the court, but the President had affirmed the sentence and dismissed the officer from the
service, The Attorney General recommended that the officer
should be nominated to the Senate for the same office, to take
rank from the date of his former commission. It is presumed the
recommendation was adopted.

PROCEEDINGS OF A GENERAL COURT MARTIAL

FOR THE

TRIAL OF BREVET BRIG. GEN. GEORGE TALCOTT,

COLONEL OF THE ORDNANCE DEPARTMENT,

Convened at Washington, June 23, 1851,

BY ORDER OF THE PRESIDENT OF THE UNITED STATES.

MAJOR GENERAL TWIGGS, *President of the Court.*
MAJOR LEE, *Judge Advocate.*

PROCEEDINGS

OF A

GENERAL COURT MARTIAL,

ASSEMBLED AT WASHINGTON CITY, D. C., BY VIRTUE OF THE FOLLOWING ORDERS:

WAR DEPARTMENT,

ADJUTANT GENERAL'S OFFICE,
Washington, June 10, 1851. 1

GENERAL ORDERS, No. 29.

A general court martial, to consist of thirteen members, will assemble in the city of Washington, D. C., at 11 o'clock, A. M., on Monday, 23d instant, or as soon thereafter as practicable, for the trial of Brevet Brigadier General George Talcott, Colonel of Ordnance.

DETAIL FOR THE COURT.

1. Brevet Major General D. E. Twiggs.
2. Brevet Major General J. E. Wool.
3. Brevet Major General P. F. Smith, Col. Mounted Riflemen. 2
4. Brevet Major General B. Riley, Colonel 1st Infantry.
5. Brevet Major General G. Gibson, Commissary General.
6. Brevet Brigadier General J. B. Walback, Col. 4th Artillery.
7. Brevet Brigadier General S. Churchill, Inspector General.
8. Brevet Brigadier General J. G. Totten, Colonel Corps of Engineers.
9. Brevet Brigadier General N. S. Clarke, Colonel 6th Infantry.
10. Brevet Brigadier General T. Childs, Major 1st Artillery.
11. Colonel J. J. Abert, Corps Topographical Engineers.
12. Colonel J. B. Crane, 1st Artillery.
13. Brevet Colonel J. Plympton, Lieut. Colonel 7th Infantry.

Brevet Major J. F. Lee, Judge Advocate.

Should any of the officers named in the detail be prevented
3 from attending at the time and place specified, the court will,
nevertheless, proceed to and continue the business before it, provided the number of members present be not less than the minimum prescribed by law.

By order of the President,

R. JONES, *Adjutant General.*

Judge Advocate.

WASHINGTON, June 23d, 1851.

The court met pursuant to the aforegoing orders. Present, all
the members named in the order, except General Clarke, where-
4 upon the court was closed, and a member stated that according
to information he had received, General Clarke was detained yesterday by an accident in Philadelphia, and might, therefore, be expected to be present to-morrow; whereupon the court decided to adjourn to meet to-morrow at 9 o'clock. The court was then opened and the adjournment announced.

---

9 o'clock, Tuesday, June 24th, 1851.

The court met pursuant to adjournment. Present, as yesterday, all the members except General Clarke.
5 The record of yesterday was read over, when the following
note was presented by General Talcott:

Mr. President and Gentlemen of Court:

The accused respectfully requests that, if consistent with the convenience of the court, the trial may not be commenced until after the arrival of the eleven o'clock train to-day, in the hope that the absent member may then arrive and a full court be organized.

G. TALCOTT, *Bt. Brig. Gen'l,*
Colonel of Ordnance.

6 Upon which application the court was closed and decided to
take a recess till 12 o'clock this day in expectation of General Clarke's arrival, whereupon the court was opened and adjourned.

12 o'clock Tuesday, June 24th, 1851.

The court met again pursuant to adjournment. Present, all
the members named in the order except General Clarke; General
Talcott also present in court. The court then proceeded to or-
ganize. General Talcott, having heard read on yesterday the
general order constituting the court, was now enquired of by
7 the Judge Advocate if he had any objection to any member named
therein, to which he replied in the negative. The court was then sworn in his presence by the Judge Advocate, according to due form of law, and the Judge Advocate was duly sworn by the presiding officer of the court, and General Talcott was then arraigned on the following charges and specifications to wit:

Charges and specifications to charges preferred against Brevet Brigadier General George Talcott, Colonel of the Ordnance Department, by order of the Secretary of War.

CHARGE 1.—*Violation of the 132d article of the regulations for the government of the Ordnance Department.* 8

Specification—In this, that he, the said Brevet Brigadier General George Talcott, Colonel of the Ordnance Department, in
charge of the Ordnance Bureau of the War Department, did,
without the sanction of the Secretary of War, at Washington,
November 6th, 1850, write and transmit by the hands of Doctor
Edward Carmichael to Brevet Colonel Benjamin Huger, a Captain
in the Ordnance Department, commanding the Arsenal at Fort 9
Monroe, the following letter of instructions, to wit:

ORDNANCE DEPARTMENT,
Washington, 6th November, 1850.

COLONEL B. HUGER, *Fort Monroe Arsenal:*

Sir,—It may be well to provide more shot and shells, from
time to time, for the post of Fort Monroe, and for this purpose
you are authorized to procure them to a reasonable extent if as
I suppose, (the price of iron being now so low,) they can be had 10
on favorable terms. You will make the necessary estimates of
funds to meet the deliveries as they occur. They should be procured by open purchase only.

I am, sir, your ob't servant,
(Signed) G. TALCOTT,
Bt. Brig. Gen'l, Colonel of Ordnance.

And on the receipt whereof the said Benjamin Huger, having
on the 8th November, 1850, at Fort Monroe Arsenal, given to the
said Doctor Carmichael an order in writing as follows: 11

FORT MONROE ARSENAL,
November 8th, 1850.

DOCTOR EDWARD CARMICHAEL:

Sir,—You will please furnish the Ordnance Department with five hundred tons 32 pdr. solid shot, at such times within one year from this date, as shall be practicable, to be delivered on the Ordnance Wharf, at Fort Monroe, subject to inspection and free of all cost to the United States.

For the shot, when inspected, will be paid three cents, three 12
and one-fourth mills per pound, (3 cents 3-4 mills) with the understanding that the department may, at any time within the year specified, order and receive from you shot and shells of any calibre, in any quantities not exceeding five hundred tons, at the above named price for shot, and at the rate of four cents and one-fourth of a mill per pound (4 cents 1 1-4 mill) for shells.

Respectfully, your ob't serv't,
(Signed) BENJ. HUGER, *Bt. Colonel.*

Which order the said Carmichael did then and there accept,
and upon the terms and conditions thereof did contract with said
Huger for shot and shells; and the said Huger having thereafter,
13 that is to say, on the 21st November, 1850, at Washington, communicated to the said George Talcott, Colonel of the Ordnance
Department, that he had, under the instructions contained in the
aforesaid letter from said Talcott, dated the 6th November, 1850,
given the said order to said Carmichael, and upon the terms and
conditions thereof, concluded a contract with said Carmichael,
he, the said Talcott, did allow and approve the said act of said
Huger, thereby permitting and sanctioning a contract for supplies to be made and carried into effect without the sanction
14 of the Secretary of War, and in violation of the 132d article of
the regulations for the government of the Ordnance Department.

CHARGE 2d.—*Wilful disobedience of orders and instructions from the Secretary of War, in relation to a contract for supplies.*

Specification—In this, that he, the said Brevet Brigadier General
George Talcott, Colonel of the Ordnance Department, in charge
of the Ordnance Bureau of the War Department, having accompanied Doctor Edward Carmichael to the War Department, on
the 1st November, 1850, and being then and there present in his
15 official capacity, when said Carmichael presented to the Secretary of War an application for a contract to furnish shot and
shells to the Ordnance Department, and when said Secretary did
then and there reject said application, and refuse to make a contract with said Carmichael, and did, moreover, refuse to recognize one which said Carmichael alleged to have been previously
made with him, nevertheless, he, the said Talcott, did afterwards,
that is to say, on the 6th November, 1850, at Washington, write
and send by the hands of said Carmichael to Brevet Colonel Ben-
16 jamin Huger, a Captain in the Ordnance Department, commanding the arsenal at Fort Monroe, the letter of instructions herein-
before recited in the specification to the just charge, with the
design and purpose to authorize and procure for said Carmichael
a contract for shot and shells; and thereby to evade and disobey
the aforesaid decision of the Secretary of War; by which means
the said Carmichael did procure from said Huger the order and
contract for shot and shells set forth in the said specification to the
1st charge. And the said Talcott being thereafter, to wit: at
Washington, on the 21st of November, 1850, informed by said
17 Huger of said contract, and well knowing that the same was
contrary to the decision of the Secretary of War, in regard to
which decision he, the said Talcott, was duly informed and instructed by the said Secretary, nevertheless, he, the said Talcott,
did allow and sanction said contract made by said Huger with
said Carmichael; therein, and in these premises, violating his
duty and disobeying the orders and instructions of the Secretary
of War.

CHARGE 3d.—*Conduct unbecoming an officer and a gentleman.*

Specification 1st—In this, that he, the said Brevet Brigadier
General George Talcott, Colonel of the Ordnance Department, 18
in charge of the Ordnance Bureau of the War Department, did
by the means and contrivances set out in the specification to
the 1st charge, and in the specification to the 2d charge, that
is to say, by his letter of instructions to Brevet Colonel Huger
of the 6th November, 1850, sent by the hands of Doctor Carmichael, and by his subsequent approval of the contract made by
said Huger with said Carmichael, authorize and procure, and
cause to be made, a contract for the purchase of a large amount
of ordnance stores, to wit: shot and shells, which he, the said Tal- 19
cott, knew, and had previously reported to the Secretary of War,
were not needed for the public service; such conduct being an
abuse of the authority of his office, a breach of the trust reposed
in him, and unbecoming an officer and a gentleman.

Specification 2d—In this, that he, the said Brevet Brigadier
General George Talcott, Colonel of the Ordnance Department,
in charge of the Ordnance Bureau of the War Department, did,
by the means and contrivances aforesaid, that is to say, by his
aforesaid letter of the 6th November, 1850, to Brevet Colonel
Huger, sent by the hands of Doctor Carmichael, and by his sub- 20
sequent consent to the contract aforesaid, made by said Huger
with said Carmichael, authorize and procure, and cause to be
made, and did confirm a contract for a large amount of ordnance
stores, to wit: shot and shells, with a person, that is to say, with
said Carmichael, who, as he, the said Talcott, believed and knew
was not in a capacity to execute the said contract, and did not
intend to execute it otherwise than through a sale or assignment
of the contract to some other person; thereby wilfully and
knowingly exposing the government to loss, and the public 21
service under his charge to the discredit arising from the sale of
a public contract; in consequence whereof a contract was made,
which was subsequently sold and transferred for a large sum, to
wit: six thousand five hundred dollars, and by which contract
the government was made liable to pay for certain shot and
shells more by that amount that it would have paid for the same
by a contract made directly with the manufacturer; such conduct
being an abuse of his official authority, a breach of the trust reposed in him, and unbecoming an officer and a gentleman.

Specification 3d—In this, that the said Brevet Brigadier Gen- 22
eral George Talcott, Colonel of the Ordnance Department, in
charge of the Ordnance Bureau of the War Department, well
knowing of the aforesaid contract with Doctor Carmichael, and
that said Carmichael had engaged J. R. Anderson (proprietor of
the Tredegar Iron Works in Richmond) to execute the said contract, and well knowing his official duty not to conceal, but to
make known such contract to the Secretary of War, did, nevertheless, wilfully and designedly conceal it, and all knowledge

thereof, from the Secretary of War, from the 21st November,
1850, to the 11th April, 1851, and more particularly in the following instances and occasions, that is to say: on the 18th Jan-
23 uary, 1851, when the Secretary of War did inquire of him at the
War Department, and did then and there endeavor to ascertain
from him whether the aforesaid Tredegar Works in Richmond
had a contract for making shot or shells for the Ordnance Department: and again on the 22d January, 1851, in written report
from the Ordnance Bureau made by his, the said Talcott's, order,
to the Secretary of War, in answer to a call from the said Secretary for information of all existing contracts chargeable upon the
appropriations for the armament of fortifications, and for ord-
24 nance, and ordnance stores and supplies: and again on the
27th January, 1851, in a written report of that date made to the
Secretary of War on the same subject, and in reply to further inquiries from said Secretary, who was thereby again seeking to
ascertain whether any such contracts were outstanding: and
again in a personal interview with the Secretary of War at the
War Department, on the 30th January, 1851, when questioned
by said Secretary as to the meaning or intention of the aforesaid
letter to Brevet Colonel Huger, dated 6th November, 1850,
whereof a copy was enclosed in said report of the 27th January,
52 1851: and again on or about the 1st March, 1851, when the Secretary of War did again enquire of him in regard to this matter
in a personal interview at the War Department, and did endeavor
to ascertain from him whether any shot or shells were being
made for the Ordnance Department at the Tredegar Iron Works:
and again on the 10th April, at the War Department, when the
Secretary of War read to him a letter from Thomas Green, dated
5th April, 1851, alleging that the Tredegar Iron Works were
making shot and shells for the Ordnance Department under a
26 contract probably given to Doctor Carmichael, and when said
Secretary did repeat his enquiries with regard to that matter; on
which several times and occasions, he, the said Talcott, did wilfully and designedly withhold and conceal from the said Secretary
of War all knowledge of the said contract with Carmichael; such
concealment and suppression being with intent to deceive the
said Secretary, being in breach of his, the said Talcott's, official
duty, and of the trust reposed in him, and being conduct unbecoming an officer and a gentleman.

Specification 4th—In this, that he, the said Brevet Brigadier
27 General George Talcott, Colonel of the Ordnance Department,
in charge of the Ordnance Bureau of the War Department, did,
on the 18th January, 1851, at the War Department, state to the
Secretary of War, wilfully and falsely, and with intent to deceive
him, that neither the proprietors of the Tredegar Iron Works
nor any other establishment had any contract to furnish shot or
shells to the Ordnance Department; whereas, in truth and in
fact, and as the said Talcott well knew, a large contract for shot

and shells, and then outstanding, had been given to Doctor Edward Carmichael, which he had, as the said Talcott further knew, 28
engaged Joseph R. Anderson, proprietor of the Tredegar Iron Works, to execute.

Specification 5th—In this, that he, the said Brevet Brigadier General George Talcott, Colonel of the Ordnance Department, in charge of the Ordnance Bureau of the War Department, did, at the time and place therein set out, write and transmit to the Secretary of War the following report, that is to say:

ORDNANCE DEPARTMENT,
Washington, Jan. 27th, 1851. 29

HON. C. M. CONRAD, *Secretary of War:*

SIR,—In answer to the note from the War Department of this date I have to report; that no contract has been made for shot, by this Department, from the last appropriations; no shot have been furnished; there are no contracts for shot, made by this department unfulfilled; and none are now contemplated.

Supposing that the enquiry may have reference to a letter officially addressed to Bt. Col. Huger, on the 6th November, 1850. I deem it not improper to send you a copy of that letter; although not specifically called for by your note. Col. Huger's 30
estimate for the present quarter, the only one received from him since the above date, contains nothing for the purchase of shot.

Respectfully, your ob't servant,

(Signed.) G. TALCOTT,
Bt. Brig. Gen'l, Col. of Ordnance.

And, in this, further, that he the said Talcott, did a few days thereafter, to wit, on the 30th Jan, 1851, when questioned by the Secretary of War as to the meaning of the aforesaid letter to Brevet Col. Huger, dated 6th November, 1850, whereof a copy 31
was transmitted to the Secretary of War with the aforesaid report dated January 27th, 1851, did state to the said secretary, that the meaning and object of said letter to said Huger, was to enable the Commander of the Arsenal at Fort Monroe to purchase shot and shells in small quantities as they might be required from time to time for experiments and artillery practice. Which written report and explanatory oral statement were false in fact and intent, and were made with design to deceive the said Secretary of War: he, the said Talcott, well knowing that a large contract was outstanding, which had been given to Doctor Car- 32
michael for shot and shells for the Ordnance Department, which contract had no view to any provision for experiments or artillery practice; well knowing that he had permitted, allowed, and approved the said contract; well knowing that his said letter of instructions to said Huger, dated 6th November, 1850, was not so designed, and had not been so construed by said Huger as now represented by him, the said Talcott, to the Secretary of War;

and well knowing that Joseph R. Anderson, proprietor of the Tredegar Works had been engaged to execute the contract made with said Carmichael.

33 Specification 6th—" In this, that he, the said Brevet Brigadier General George Talcott, Colonel of the Ordnance Department in charge of the Ordnance Bureau of the War Department, being enquired of by the Secretary of War at the War Department, on or about the 1st March, 1851, in regard to information which had reached the said Secretary that the Tredegar Works were actually making shot and shells for the Ordnance Department, he, the said Talcott, did earnestly assure the said Secretary that there was not the slightest foundation for the said information. Which statement of said Talcott was false, and he knew it so to be;
34 well knowing the foundation of said report and the facts in the case; well knowing that the contract aforesaid had been made with Doctor Carmichael, that said Carmichael had employed Joseph R. Anderson, the proprietor of the Tredegar Works to execute it, and that the said Anderson claimed the right to execute it as the assignee or agent of said Carmichael.

Specification 7th—" In this, that he, the said Brevet Brigadier General George Talcott, Colonel of the Ordnance Department, in charge of the Ordnance Bureau of the War department, having heard read to him at the War Department on the 10th April,
35 1851, by the Secretary of War, a letter from Thomas Green, dated Washington, 5th April, 1851, alleging, among other things, that the Tredegar Iron Works were engaged in executing a large amount of work, for the delivery of shot and shells to the Ordnance Department, under a contract probably given by the Department, or its officers, to Doctor Edward Carmichael, and assigned by him to Mr. Anderson, proprietor of the said Tredegar Works, he, the said Talcott, did thereupon assert to said Secretary that 'there was not a word of truth in it,' meaning in said statement in said letter; that 'it was false from beginning to end,'
36 or words to that effect. Which declaration of said Talcott was positively and wilfully false, and intended to deceive the said Secretary of War.

By order of the Secretary of War,
J. F. LEE,
Judge Advocate of the Army.

To which charges and specifications, General Talcott pleaded "Not Guilty," and submitted the following in writing:

Mr. President and Gentlemen of the Court:

37 Desiring to interpose no obstacle to a full and fair enquiry into *the facts* upon which these charges and specifications have been constructed, I respectfully request that I may be allowed to reserve all matter touching their sufficiency in law, to be used in the discretion of counsel at the summing up of my defence; and

with this reservation I now plead, to all and singular the said charges and specifications, not guilty. 38

Appearing before you under circumstances for which I have not been prepared by any thing in the experience of my past life, I desire to entrust the defence of my honor and character upon this occasion to a professional friend here present; and to this end I request that J. M. Carlisle, Esq., a member of the bar of this city, may be allowed to attend me during the open sessions of the court under the restrictions ordinarily imposed upon counsel in Courts Martial. 24th June 1851.

(Signed) G. TALCOTT, *Bt. Brig'r Gen'l,*
Col. of Ordnance. 39

Which plea was ordered to be entered on the record, and the application for counsel allowed; and thereupon General Talcott presented to the court the following note.

Mr. President, and Gentlemen of the Court:

Before proceeding to the trial it is proper that I should make known to you that the Hon. Wm. L. Marcy, a witness deemed material to my defence, and for whom a summons was duly and seasonably issued by the Judge Advocate at my request, is not in attendance, nor has he been heard from in acknowledgement of
the subpœna, which was forwarded to him at Detroit. In the 40
event of his not appearing before the examination of the other witnesses shall have been concluded, I may be under the necessity of applying for a short delay; which, however, I trust will not be the case. In the mean time, I respectfully give this notice to the court in order that I may suffer no detriment by reason of the commencement of the trial in the absence of the witness.

(Signed) G. TALCOTT, *Bt. Brig'r Gen'l,*
Col. of Ordnance.

The Judge Advocate submitted the following note.

Mr. President:

As the facts on which these charges are based will involve a 41
long narrative by the mouths of witnesses, I propose, in order to bring the case before you in what appears to me the clearest and most easily intelligible manner, to put the facts in evidence as nearly as may be, in the order of time to which they belong, and therefore, not to examine each witness, when placed on the stand, through the whole case, but only on such point of it, as it is then intended to bring to your attention.

The defence, with a like view to facilitate the investigation, will confine their cross examination to the matter of the direct
examination; and the witness when required to testify to other 42
matter will be recalled by the prosecution. In this way, both sides expect to save time, and to bring out the case more clearly; and I state it now, that if it meets the approval of the court, such examinations as the court themselves desire to make of the witnesses, may be directed according to the same view.

(Signed) J. F. LEE, *Judge Advocate.*

Whereupon General Talcott presented the following:

43 *Mr. President:*

The accused begs leave to say to the court that so far as the suggestion of the Judge Advocate may affect him, he cheerfully accedes to it, believing that it will facilitate the investigation, which he sincerely desires may be thorough; and so conducted as to give the court the clearest understanding of the order of the facts, and of their bearing upon the respective specifications.

(Signed) G. TALCOTT, *Bt. Brig'r Gen'l,*
Col. of Ordnance.

44 Capt. *William Maynadier*, a witness for the prosecution, being sworn in due form of law, testified as follows:

Direct examination, by Judge Advocate—

Q. On what duty are you now, and since what time? *A.* I am the principal assistant to the Chief of the Ordnance Department, and have been on that duty from the 1st of February 1842, to the present time, continuously.

Q. Has Gen. Talcott been in charge of the Bureau during all that period? *A.* From the time first stated, till within a few days past.

45 *Q.* Will you state to the court what are the usual amounts and general objects of the appropriations for the armament of fortifications, and for ordnance and ordnance stores and supplies? *A.* The usual amount of each of the appropriations named is $100,000 annually. The general object of the appropriation for the armament of fortifications is to arm the fortifications of the country; and the money appropriated is applicable to the purchase of sea-coast and garrison cannon, and suitable projectiles for such cannon; of timber, iron, and other materials used in constructing sea-coast and garrison carriages, implements and equip-
46 ments; also to the payment of all expenses attending the fabrication and repairs of such articles.

The general object of the appropriation for ordnance and ordnance stores and supplies, is to provide field and siege artillery, side-arms and accoutrements for troops in the United States service. The money appropriated is applicable to the purchase of field and siege cannon, and suitable projectiles, of swords and sabres; and of iron timber, leather and other materials used in making field and siege carriages, and implements, accoutrements, ammunition and harness, and all expenses attending the fabrica-
47 tion and repairs of these articles at the arsenals.

Q. Were you in charge of the Ordnance Bureau in May 1850? *A.* During the temporary absence of Gen. Talcott, I was.

Q. Did Dr. Carmichael apply to you for any contract at that time; if yea, tell what decision was had thereon? *A.* Doctor Carmichael submitted to me certain papers from ex-President Tyler and ex-Secretary Wilkins, by virtue of which he claimed to be entitled to a contract for shot and shells. I referred him to the Secretary of War, Mr. Crawford, by whom the papers were sent to me for a report. I made a report. 48

Q. Is this an office copy of that report? *A.* It is.

The report here read as follows:

ORDNANCE DEPARTMENT,
Washington May 21st, 1850.

Hon. G. W. CRAWFORD, *Secretary of War:*

Sir—I have to acknowledge the reference to this office (for report) of certain papers relating to a claim of Dr. E. W. Carmichael to receive from Government a contract to supply shot and shells. As this claim rests on a verbal promise from the Secretary of War, during the administration of Mr. Tyler, there is of 49
course nothing on the records of this department to throw any light on it, and nothing but the papers presented by Dr. Carmichael, from which any information on the subject can be derived. From these papers it appears that Messrs. Wellford and Carmichael having completed "limited contracts" for castings, applied for a further contract to supply one thousand tons of shot and shells; that the Secretary of War, whose attention was invited to the matter by the President, expressed his intention of granting the contract as suggested, when the passage of the appropriation bill might make it legal for him to do so; that thereupon 50
Mr. Tyler stated to Messrs. Wellford and Carmichael "that they might feel themselves entirely secure in the business, and proceed to make the necessary preparations," which they did accordingly, and that the appropriation bill passed too late to permit the contract to be made during Mr. Tyler's administration. "The limited contracts" executed for the War Department by Messrs. Wellford and Carmichael during Mr. Tyler's administration (exclusive of that for the navy, mentioned in Mr. Wilkins's letter) amounted to about 294 tons of shot and shells, for which they received $29,918·94. Under the succeeding administration these gentlemen obtained 51
and executed contracts for shot and shells to the amount of more than 500 tons, for which they received $48,948·83; making together 794 tons at $78,867·77.

The government is not now in want of such supplies, and could not contract for them at this time, if it were; because there is no law or appropriation on which to base such contracts, as required by the 6th section of the act approved 1st May 1820.

The papers in the case are herewith returned.

I have the honor to be
Sir, your ob't serv't. 52
WM. MAYNADIER, *Capt. of Ordnance,*
in charge of Ordnance Department.

Direct examination of the witness continued.

Q. The words "limited contracts," used in this report, appear quoted—will you explain why, and the sense in which you designed to use the word "limited"? *A.* I quoted it from ex-Pre-

sident Tyler's letter, and used limited in rather an ironical sense;
53 thinking the contracts had been rather ample than limited.

Q. Will the witness read the law of the 1st May 1820, to which in his report he refers the Secretary of War? *A.* The law read as follows, at 207th page of Cross, and in 6th section of that act:

Sec. 6. And be it further enacted, that no contract shall hereafter be made by the Secretary of State, or of the Treasury, or of the Department of War, or of the Navy, except under a law authorizing the same, or under an appropriation adequate to its fulfillment; and excepting, also, contracts for the subsistence and clothing of the Army or Navy, and contracts by the Quarter-
54 Master's Department, which may be made by the Secretaries of those Departments.

Direct examination, continued.

Q, Is this paper here exhibited to witness the decision of the Secretary of War, Mr. Crawford, as transmitted from the War Department to the Ordnance Bureau, for file? *A.* It is.

The following paper was exhibited to witness, with the question last preceding:

War Department,
Washington, May 23d, 1850.

55 Sir,—From the examination given to the papers which you handed to me, a few days since, it appears that during the year 1844 yourself and partner entered into a contract with the Government to furnish shot and shells to the amount of about $30,000. The satisfactory manner in which you executed this contract induced the then President, and Secretary of War, to promise another of larger amount, but the restriction of the Act of Congress, May 1st, 1820, interposed an obstacle, so long as an appropriation, applicable to the object, was withheld or postponed by Congress. This appropriation was passed, but so late that no
56 time was permitted to put it in valid form, the promise to which I have adverted.

These gentlemen, lately connected with the Government, exerted their influence to obtain, in part or whole, a recognition of their verbal promises made to you, by recommending, in 1845, yourself and partner to the favorable consideration of the Department, and giving a statement of what had occurred in relation to the contract intended to be entered into between yourselves and the Government. The late Secretary of War immediately thereafter contracted with you to deliver 500 tons of shot and shell equal in value to about $79,000. On this statement of the facts,
57 I infer from the letter of a legal adviser, which accompanies your papers, that you desire to be indemnified against loss sustained, in consequence of the non-fulfillment of the verbal promises before mentioned. As a question of damages, the Department can not decide it, without additional legislation.

If, however, the past transaction be considered as constituting a claim on the Government to make a contract, by which the

informal agreement of our predecessors may be carried into effect,
I have then to refer you to the enclosed report from the Ord- 58
nance Bureau, and to say whenever the means are granted, the
ordinary and legal mode of making contracts will be pursued.

I am, very respectfully, your ob't servant,

GEO. W. CRAWFORD,
Secretary of War.

Dr. E. H. Carmichael.

Direct examination, resumed.

Q. When did Dr. Carmichael next again apply for a contract,
if you know? *A*. I don't know that he came again and applied
for a contract. There is no record of such subsequent application in our office. I was absent from the office from the 16th of 59
October to the 11th of November, and when I returned he was
not here.

The defence had no cross-examination to make at this time, and
the witness retired.

Charles M. Conrad, Secretary of War, a witness for the prosecutor, being sworn in due form of law, testified as follows:

Direct examination, by Judge Advocate—

Q. Did Dr. Carmichael apply to you, as Secretary of War, for
a contract in the fall of 1850? if yea, will you state to the Court
what passed on that subject. *A*. Some time about the latter
end of October, or early in November last, General Talcott came 60
into my office at the War Department, shortly after I reached it
in the morning, accompanied by a gentleman whom he introduced
to me as Dr. Carmichael, of Virginia. After the gentleman was
seated, General Talcott told me that Dr. Carmichael wished to
speak to me on some business which he had with the Department,
and which he, Dr. Carmichael, would explain. Dr. Carmichael
then observed that he came to see me in relation to a contract
for making shot. He said that he had made a contract for a
considerable quantity of shot with some previous head of the
Department. I do not recollect what individual he spoke of as 61
the head of the Department, or whether he mentioned his name.
But that the officer had left office before the contract was executed, and therefore the contract had never been fulfilled—that he
had applied, however, to Mr. Crawford, my immediate predecessor,
to carry out the contract, and that Mr. Crawford had recognized
it; but had also left office before the contract was executed; and
he called upon me now to allow him to execute the contract.

I asked him if he had the contract, or if it was in writing, I
forget which. He stated that it was not in writing, but that it
was fully understood, and that Mr. Crawford was satisfied of the
existence of the contract, and recognized its validity. I asked if 62
he had any evidence of that recognition. He said the papers in
the case would show it. General Talcott, who was present
during this conversation, had a bundle of papers in his hand. I
asked, addressing myself to him—"General are those the papers?"
He said they were. He was seated near me, and I requested him
to hand them to me, which he did. I examined the papers to

look simply for the recognition of Mr. Crawford. I found this
63 paper, (the letter of Mr. Crawford, addressed to Dr. Carmichael, entered at page of the record here shown to witness) which I read over attentively, and after doing so I observed to Dr. Carmichael, that, according to that paper, it seemed to me that Mr. Crawford, so far from acknowledging or recognizing the existence of any contract on the part of the Government, expressly and positively negatived its existence. The Dr. said he thought differently; and I then read to him the last clause of Mr. Crawford's letter in which he refers him to the report of the Ordnance Bureau, and says to him that when the means are granted, the
64 ordinary and legal mode of making contracts would be pursued. This clause, I said to Dr. Carmichael, appeared to me utterly inconsistent with the *recognition* of a contract, and on the contrary to say that when a contract should be given, it would be according to the legal mode, which I said, I understood to be by inviting proposals. The Dr. still contended for some time that his view of the letter was correct, and also stated that there was a verbal understanding between himself and Mr. Crawford, by which he was to make the shot.

In answer to that, I told him that I had adopted as a rule ever
65 since I had been in the Department, having been frequently called upon to recognize verbal promises or agreements, made by or with my predecessors, to recognize nothing as binding that did not appear on the records of the Departments, or in writing. The Dr. made a very earnest appeal to me to be allowed to make some shot; and presented a good many, (of what he seemed to regard as arguments or considerations likely to influence me) to induce me to allow him to make some shot. But I persisted in my refusal in very positive terms; and he left the office somewhat dissatisfied at my decision.

96 *Q.* Did you state any other reason than those mentioned, any reason having reference to the state of the public supplies, why you would not give a contract for shot? *A.* My impression is, and it is very strong, that I stated to him that the department was not at that time in want of shot, or was not making shot, on that point however I will not be positive.

Q. Did General Talcott make any remark, or offer any suggestion to the Secretary of War, at any time, during this conversation, either in regard to the facts stated by Dr. Carmichael, or to the wants of the public service, if so be pleased to state them.
67 *A.* My recollection is, Sir, that during the conversation Gen. Talcott remained silent; indeed I was somewhat surprised after I discovered that there was no recognition of the contract by Mr. Crawford, that Gen. Talcott had allowed the statement of Dr. Carmichael on that point to pass uncontradicted. I thought of it after he left the room as a singular circumstance, and but for the accidental circumstance of my calling for the papers and

examining them there, I should have taken the fact as certain,
being as I am in the habit of receiving as evidence of fact every 68
report and statement made to me by the head of a bureau, I was
the more surprised from the fact, that a day or two after Gen.
Talcott came into the office, on other business, and introduced the
subject of the conversation with Dr. Carmichael, and observed to
me, in speaking of that conversation, "You were right, there
never was any recognition of the contract," and spoke as I
thought somewhat sneeringly of Dr. Carmichael's declarations
that there had been such recognition.

Q. Can you fix more nearly than you have stated the *date* of
this conversation? *A.* No I only fix it by the time of my return 69
from New York. I returned on the 23rd and resumed the business of
the office on the 24th. I know that the conversation occurred a
short time, a few days, after my return.

The Judge Advocate stated that he rested the direct examination of this witness here for the present.

Cross examination, by defence—

Q. Did Gen. Talcott perform any other office, or take any
other part in the interview between yourself and Dr. Carmichael
than that of introducing that person to you, and stating that he,
Carmichael, desired to see you upon some business, as to which 70
he could speak for himself? *A.* Nothing—I have stated what
occurred.

Q. Are you clear in your recollection that Gen. Talcott had the bundle of papers in his hand when you called for them; or did he merely pass them to you from Carmichael? *A.* He had them in his possession.

Q. Did you remark whether he brought them in with him, or
whether Dr. Carmichael handed them to him during the interview, and if so, at what period of the interview? *A.* My impression is, that he brought them in, I do not recollect seeing 71
Charmichael give them.

Q. Was there any thing said by Carmichael as to the time or place when a verbal recognition of the contract had been made, and did he say Gen. Talcott was present, or had any knowledge of it? *A.* I do not recollect that any thing of the kind was said as to the time or place, or as to Gen. Talcott's having knowledge of it.

Q. Was there any cause for surprise then, that Gen. Talcott
did not contradict the statement that a verbal recognition had
been given by the Secretary, of which he could have no know- 72
ledge? *A.* My remark about my surprise applied more particularly to the assertion that it had been recognized in writing,
but I also attach some importance to the declaration made in
Gen. Talcott's presence that it had been verbally recognized.
The matter relating to an affair of his bureau, and the declaration made positively in his presence, I might have presumed it to

be correct, and acted on that presumption, as I have stated, I am
73 in the habit of receiving the declarations or admissions of the heads of bureaus with implicit confidence.

Q. As to the alleged written recognition, was it not one of the papers which you say were handed to you by Gen. Talcott, and was there any commentary from him necessary to make it intelligible to you? *A.* I have already stated that my looking at the papers at all was entirely accidental; if Gen. Talcott had himself stated that such a contract existed, I should have taken the fact for granted, as I am in the daily habit of doing in reference to contracts made by all the heads of bureaux, and when
74 Dr. Carmichael made the assertion in his presence, and he remained silent, I considered it at the time as equivalent to making the declaration himself, or nearly so, and I took the papers with an entire conviction that I should find in them a recognition of the contract by Mr. Crawford, and was a good deal surprised when I found it was not so.

And here at the hour of three the court adjourned, to meet tomorrow at nine o'clock.

---

75 9 o'clock, Wednesday, June 25th, 1851.

The court met pursuant to adjournment. Present all the members as yesterday organized, the Judge Advocate and Gen. Talcott.

Charles M. Conrad, Secretary of War, a witness of the prosecution in continuation.

Cross examination, resumed:

Q. You stated in your direct examination yesterday, that when you asked Mr. Carmichael if he had any evidence of the recognition of his contract, he answered that *the papers* in the case would
76 shew it, and that you thereupon asked General Talcott if the papers he held in his hand were the papers in the case, to which he answered that they were, and handed them to you upon your request; have you now any knowledge that the said papers which according to your recollection were handed to you by General Talcott, were other or less than the true papers, and all the papers, necessary to the decision of the question whether such recognition had in fact and law been made? *A.* I have no such knowledge.

Q. You have stated that the said "bundle of papers" contained
77 the decision of Mr. Secretary Crawford upon the validity of the said alleged contract; *are you able to state what other papers it contained?* *A.* I do not think that I examined any one paper in the package, except the letter of Mr. Crawford referred to in my testimony of yesterday; I took up *that* because I saw the name of Mr. Crawford appended to it; I asked Dr. Carmichael if that was the recognition that he spoke of, and he said it was; he never alluded to any other paper than the one in question.

Q. When Mr. Carmichael answered your inquiry as to the evidence of recognition of his contract, by saying that the papers 78
in the case would show it, what led you to ask Gen. Talcott immediately "are those the papers? *A*. I presume I was led to ask that question, because the idea occurred to me that if those were the papers I would look at the recognition spoken of.

Q. What I desire to understand is, whether the fact that the package of papers was there held openly before you, did not naturally lead you to infer that they were the papers in the case? *A*. It did.

Q. If General Talcott *brought with him* and *held conspicuously in his hand before you*, the papers touching Carmichael's claim, 79
and amongst them a clear written decision against it by Mr. Crawford, could you suppose that he meant knowingly to endorse an untruth, the *means of exposing which, he* himself at the same time, as you say, held openly under your eye, in such manner as to lead you to understand that it was the paper referred to? *A*. I did not say that he held the papers conspicuously before me so as to invite my attention to them, or that he opened any papers to me; he held the package of papers in his hand, and I asked him if those were the papers; with this explanation of the facts, I proceed to answer the question, and say that upon the supposition 80
that I would examine the papers, such a design is not supposable; but upon the supposition that I might not examine the papers, such a design is perfectly consistent with the fact of having the papers in his hand.

Q. Can you suggest a reason why General Talcott should have brought those papers before you, (if he did,) while he meant to give countenance to an assertion plainly refuted by them? *A*. I could only give suspicions; I do not know that I can with propriety give them, unless the court or the gentlemen desire to hear them; I know no facts; I do not mean that I had no suspicions 81
then; the suspicions I now refer to arose subsequently; I mean that I then thought the part taken by General Talcott strange and singular, but my view of it then did not cause what may be called suspicions; it struck me as singular, and the more I reflected upon it, the more it struck me in that light; it made an impression on my memory; it struck me as strange at the time, and more so in consequence of what General Talcott afterwards said on that subject.

Q. Did Dr. Carmichael make any other application to you at the interview in question, than that which you have specified, 82
viz: to redeem the pledge which he alleged the former government had made him? *A*. Dr. Carmichael urged upon me to allow him to make a quantity of shot, partly on the ground of a positive contract, and partly on account of equitable considerations which he mentioned, such as his having made arrangements to comply with what he claimed to be a contract, and he urged me by many arguments and persuasions, as other people do when

soliciting contracts; among other things he said he was going to
83 reside in my city, New Orleans; I was inflexible, however, and perhaps shewed some little impatience, as I thought he had endeavored to practice a deception upon me, and finally he gave up in despair.

Q. Be pleased to state at what time you left this city in the fall of 1850? *A.* I think I was gone about a fortnight or 20 days; I do not recollect the precise time; I returned on the 23d, as the records of the department show that I resumed official business on the 24th.

Cross examination here ended.

84 *Question by the court*—

Q. Was there anything in the circumstances inconsistent with the supposition that General Talcott, after Dr. Carmichael had finished his argument, would, at that interview, have given the opinion he afterwards expressed, viz: that there was no pledge in Mr. Crawford's letter, provided you, in the mean time, had not come to the same opinion by the perusal of Mr. Crawford's letter? *A.* The reason why my surprise at General Talcott's silence, when Dr. Carmichael asserted that there was a written recognition of the contract by Mr. Crawford, was increased by
85 his remarking at a subsequent interview, "that I was right in deciding that there was no recognition," was this: I had supposed it possible that General Talcott agreed with Dr. Carmichael in supposing that Mr. Crawford's letter amounted to a recognition of the contract; but when he afterwards said that he agreed with me that there was no such recognition, my surprise at his silence increased because I did not know how to account for it.

Captain William Maynadier, witness for the prosecution, recalled.

Question by Judge Advocate—

86 *Q.* In making your report to Mr. Secretary Crawford, dated 21st May, 1850, against Carmichael's claim, were you acquainted with General Talcott's opinion on this subject? *A.* I don't recollect ever to have heard General Talcott express an opinion on that subject prior to the date of that report, but I think that on his return in last year, in June, 1850, I brought that report to his attention as showing what I had done in Carmichael's case, I am not positive, but it is my impression, and that he approved what I had done; I am sure that he read my report in March of this year, and expressed to me his approbation.

87 *Cross examination*—

Q. Has not that report stood from that day to this as the official report of the Ordnance Department, upon Dr. Carmichael's claim? *A.* It has so stood.

Re-examined—

Q. Do you know that any other subsequent occasion arose for any report or other official action of the bureau in that matter, before Dr. Carmichael brought up the case to Mr. Conrad last fall? *A.* I do not. 88

The Judge Advocate submitted the following note:

I now propose that the defence admit that Dr. Carmichael, as shown by the books at Willard's Hotel, was in this city on the 30th and 31st of October, 1850, and that he is there entered as having gone on the 31st of October to other lodgings.

Whereupon General Talcott offered the following note:

"The accused supposing the Judge Advocate's information to be correct, admits the facts to be as stated." 89

Brevet Colonel Benjamin Huger, a Captain in the Ordnance Department, a witness on the part of the prosecution, being sworn in due form of law, testified as follows:

Direct examination, by Judge Advocate.

Q. Will you relate to the Court the facts and circumstances attending your giving Dr. Carmichael, in November last, an order to furnish supplies to the Ordnance Department? *A.* Very early in November last, Dr, Carmichael came to Fort Monroe, I understood from Washington, and stated to me—

Here the defence interposed the following objections: 90

The accused objects to any testimony being given as to declarations or statements by Dr. Carmichael of the purport or scope of which statements or declarations, he, the accused, not being present, can have no knowledge; and which are clearly incompetent to affect him in any manner.

G. TALCOTT,
Bt. Brig. Gen'l, Colonel Ordnance.

The Judge Advocate enquired of the witness whether what Dr. Carmichael then stated to him, was by him, witness, ever made known to General Talcott. Witness could not distinctly 91
remember, thought he had made it known to him.

The Judge Advocate waived for the present demanding of witness to state what Carmichael said.

Witness resumed—On his application I furnished him a list of such shot as I thought it advantageous to the service should be procured at Fort Monroe. On the 8th day of November Dr. Carmichael returned to Fort Monroe, bringing me this letter from General Talcott, written and signed by his hand:

ORDNANCE DEPARTMENT,
Washington, 6th November, 1850. 92

COL. B. HUGER, *Commanding Fort Monroe Arsenal:*

Sir,—It may be well to provide more shot and shells, from time to time, for the post of Fort Monroe, and for this purpose you are authorized to procure them to a reasonable extent if, as I suppose (the price of iron being now so low,) they can be had on favorable terms. You will make the necessary estimates of funds to meet the deliveries as they occur. They should be procured by open purchase only.

I am, sir, respectfully,
Your obedient servant,
G. TALCOTT,
Bt. Brig. General, Col. of Ordnance.

93 Witness continued—On receipt of this letter from General Talcott, I gave Dr. Carmichael an order as follows:

FORT MONROE ARSENAL,
November 8th, 1850.

DR. EDWARD CARMICHAEL:

Sir,—You will please furnish the Ordnance Department with five hundred tons 32 pdr. solid shot, at such times, within one year from this date, as shall be practicable, to be delivered on
94 the Ordnance Wharf, at Fort Monroe, subject to inspection, and free of all cost to the United States.

For the shot, when inspected, will be paid three cents three and one-fourth mills per pound, (3 cents $3\frac{1}{4}$ths,) with the understanding that the department may, at any time within the year specified, order and receive from you, shot and shells of any calibre, in any quantities not exceeding five hundred tons, at the above named price for shot, and at the rate of four cents and one-fourth of a mill per pound (4 cents $\frac{1}{4}$ mill) for shells.

Respectfully, your ob't serv't,
95 (Signed) B. HUGER, *Brevet Colonel.*

Witness resumed—One reason why I was induced to give him this order was, that I had formerly got shells from a foundry near Fredericksburg, in which he had an interest, on similar terms in regard to inspections at the fort, and he told me that they were to be made at that foundry. Dr. Carmichael brought me a memorandum in the handwriting of Mr. Adler, a clerk in the Ordnance Department, whose handwriting I knew, showing the
96 lowest prices paid for shot by the Bureau. It was a mere memorandum. I do not know what became of it; I think it purported to state the lowest prices paid for shot and shells generally without regard to calibres. That price I offered Dr. Carmichael. He proposed to add the cost of freight from Fredericksburg to Fort Monroe; we calculated it and added it in. By the next mail I received a letter from Mr. Adler, stating that, on further examination of the books, he found some shot had been purchased at a less rate, which letter came after Dr. Carmichael had left. I
97 came to Washington about the middle of November. A few days after my arrival here, General Talcott referred to me a letter from Goeuvernur Kemble to him, dated November 17th, which is here presented to the court. I am not certain how or when I received this letter; I think it was sent to me; I think Brevet

Major Talcott, of the Ordnance Department, brought it to me. I was told it was referred to me to be answered, as I gave the order.

The letter here read as follows:

(*Private.*) 98

Cold Spring, 17*th November*, 1850.

Dear General,—Dr. Carmichael, of Richmond, has written to
me enclosing a copy of a letter from Colonel Huger ordering five
hundred tons of 32 pdr. shot deliverable at Old Point Comfort,
offering the order to me for our execution and delivery according
to the terms therein specified. Of course the Doctor is to take
the lion's share of profits, but it would enable me to keep our
moulders together during the winter, when the work of the de- 99
partment generally falls off, and therefore, if an arrangement by
which the order should be transferred to me would meet the
approbation of the department, I should try to make one with
him. I shall write to him to this effect, more particularly because
there appears to be some irregularity in the transaction that I do
not understand; and I would ask the favor of you to inform me
as early as possible whether there would be any objection on your
part, and if not, how I had best arrange with him, whether
through a special power of attorney from him, or by transfer of
the order in any other manner. 100

Very sincerely, yours,

GOUV. KEMBLE.

Please direct to the care of
Wm. Kemble, New-York,

Gen'l Talcott, *Ordnance Dep't, Washington.*

Witness resumed—I answered the letter of Mr. Kemble. Here is a copy of my answer.

The answer was shown to General Talcott before it was sent,
and that was the first occasion of consultation between us on that
subject. 101

The copy produced by witness here read to the court as follows, by consent:

Washington, *November* 21*st*, 1850.

To Gouvr. Kemble, Esq'r:

My dear sir,—General Talcott has referred your letter of the
17th instant to me. Neither General T. or myself consider
the order to Dr. Carmichael, for a supply of shot, assignable in
the manner he proposes. Dr. Carmichael was interested in a
foundry near Fredericksburg, Va., and supplies of shot and 102
shells for Fort Monroe have heretofore been procured there. In
giving him the order, a copy of which he sent you, it was understood that the work was to be done at that foundry, which could only turn them out in limited quantities as required, and as I had

means to pay for them. I was authorized by General Talcott to estimate for funds to pay for them, from time to time, as I requir-
103 ed them, and my stating the whole amount that would be required was for the purpose of letting the founder (Mr. Wellford, who Dr. C. told me would have charge of the work,) make his arrangements for materials, &c., not that I expected him to deliver the whole amount immediately. Under these circumstances I am not authorized to consent to the transfer of the order to Dr. C. in the manner he proposes.

I am, very truly, yours,

(Signed) BENJ. HUGER.

(True copy) Benj. Huger.

104 Witness resumed—The General agreed with me that it was a proper answer. I considered him as approving my objection therein to the transfer. The General did remark to me that the Secretary of War would be incensed, and justly so, if an order for supplies should be hawked about in market. He also did express surprise at the amount of the order; but I did not understand him as reproving me for giving an order in compliance with his instructions. A few days after I received a letter from Brevet Captain Stone, who was in temporary command of the Arsenal at Fort Monroe during my absence, of the contents of which I
105 informed General Talcott. An extract from Captain Stone's letter of 22d November, 1850, here read, with a letter enclosed therein, which Captain Stone had received from Mr. Anderson, dated November 20th. These papers read as follows:

Fort Monroe, *November 22d*, 1850.

My dear Colonel:

I enclose you a treasury draft with the necessary papers to sign. This morning brought me a letter from Mr. Anderson, enclosing a power of attorney from Dr. Carmichael, for making
106 the shot ordered at Wellford's foundry. Is not that a beautiful operation for the Doctor? He said most expressly that he wanted the contract for the sole purpose of starting the foundry; and now he has turned the whole order over to the Tredegar Works. Shall I put the power of attorney on file and send up the guages as Anderson requests, &c. &c. &c.

Yours very truly, STONE.

Tredegar Iron Works,
November 20th, 1850.

107 Colonel B. Huger, *U. S. Army, Old Pt.*-

Dear Sir,—I enclose a power of attorney from Dr. E. H. Carmichael to attend to his order for shot. Be good enough to place it on file and to send me the necessary 32 pdr. guages.

I am, with much respect, your ob't servant,

J. R. ANDERSON.

The witness resumed—On the receipt of these papers I wrote to Captain Stone, on consultation with General Talcott, stating my objections to Dr. Carmichael's transferring the order, in con- 108
sequence of which I ascertained, after my return to Fort Monroe, Captain Stone wrote to Mr. Anderson a letter of which I present a copy from the books of the arsenal.

The letter of Captain Stone of November 26th here read as follows, by consent, from the copy:

FORT MONROE ARSENAL,
November 26th, 1850.

J. R. ANDERSON, Esq., *Tredegar Iron Works:*

Sir,—I am instructed by Colonel Huger, now in Washington, 109
to return to you the power of attorney issued to you by Dr. E. Carmichael, and to say that he (Colonel H.) thinks Dr. Carmichael had, *under the circumstances*, no right to transfer his order for shot without first consulting him and obtaining his consent.

Very respectfully, &c.,

(Signed) C. P. STONE, *Bt. Captain.*

True copy.

Witness resumed—I had no further consultations with Gen. Talcott on that matter before I returned to Fort Monroe. On 110
my return, I wrote myself to Mr Anderson.

The accused here objected, that what subsequently passed between Anderson and the witness was not admissible in evidence, unless it had been brought to the knowledge of the accused.

The Judge Advocate stated he proposed to prove the execution of the contract and the delivery of shot under it. The witness has proved, without objection, what Capt. Stone wrote to Anderson in regard to the contract, under the witness's instructions. It is proposed to prove what witness wrote to Anderson in that matter. The accused submitted the following objections in writing:

The accused begs leave to state to the court, that so far as what 111
passed between Col. Huger and Mr. Anderson, or other persons, was brought to the knowledge of the accused, and approved by him, it is admitted to be competent evidence, but no further. What Mr. Anderson wrote to Col. Huger, and what Col Huger replied, is as the accused is advised incompetent to be given in evidence, unless it were in pursuance of previous instructions from the accused, or was subsequently ratified and adopted by him.

The charges to which this testimony is supposed to apply, are the first and second.

The essence of these charges is that the accused made or pro- 112
cured, or authorized to be made, or ratified and allowed when made, a certain contract in violation of the 132d Art. of Ordnance Regulation, and in violation of orders and instructions for the Secretary of War relating thereto. The evidence thus far has

shown an official letter dated 6th Nov. 1850, from the accused to Col. Huger. authorizing him to make purchases from time to time to a reasonable extent; that Col. Huger acting upon his own
113 construction of that letter, gave an order to Dr. Carmichael; that Carmichael virtually transferred it to Anderson; that Col. Huger and the accused repudiated that transfer. How can the fact that shot were delivered, or that they were accepted by Col. Huger, affect the queston whether the *accused* made, authorized or ratified a contract in violation of the regulation and orders.

The question is not what was done, but what was done by the order, procurement or consent of the accused.

(Signed) G. TALCOTT, *Bt. Brig'r Gen'l,*
Col. of Ordnanoe.

114 The Judge Advocate said, "I propose to prove the execution of the contract under authority received from accused. Gen. Talcott is charged in one of the specifications with permitting a contract to be made and carried into effect. The authority to witness to make the contract is in proof, the knowledge thereof by accused afterwards, and the whole matter referred to witness and entrusted to him, with approval of his objections to a transfer of the contract.

Under this authority from accused to witness, it is now proposed to show that the contract was carried into effect, not re-
115 pudiated, in part executed, shot delivered, received, inspected, all that passed between Anderson and witness in regard to the recognition or repudiation of the contract, passed in writing, and the writings are the proofs.

The court closed and came to the following decision.

The court without laying down general rules for the admission of testimony will hear any objection to particular questions or answers.

The court is further of opinion that it is competent for the prosecution to introduce testimony showing the carrying into effect
116 or execution of the order or contract.

The court was then opened and the decision announced.

The direct examination of the witness resumed:

Q. State all that occurred in regard to the execution of the contract? *A.* I do not consider that the contract was executed on my part. I declined it in the answer written by Capt. Stone; I mean his letter of the 26th November.

Q. You say Capt. Stone wrote by your instructions declining it. Did you write yourself? *A.* I did write to Mr. Anderson on that subject, but never revoked the official order sent by Capt.
117 Stone of 26th November.

Q. Is not this letter here shown you a letter from you to Mr. Anderson, written on the 6th December, soon after your return to the fort, on the subject of that contract?

A letter from witness to Anderson, dated the 6th December, 1850, here shown witness.

The accused presented the following objection:

The accused now respectfully renews the objection last made by him, and applied it specifically to the correspondence between 118
the witness and Anderson now offered in evidence. If, under any circumstances, it could be received against him, it is clearly not admissible since the witness has stated that he never revoked the official letter written by his order, and with the approval of the accused.

If the object of the Judge Advocate is to contradict the statement of the witness adduced by him, it is equally inadmissible.

(Signed) G. TALCOTT,
Bt. Brig. General, Col. of Ordnance.

The Judge Advocate said, the prosecution is not concluded by 119
the statement made by their own witness, but may bring evidence to prove any material fact in the case to be otherwise their own witness believes and states it to be. With the highest respect for this witness, the prosecution may show that he is mistaken. When the witness says that he never consented to execute the contract on his part; that he never revoked his official letter, written on his part, by Captain Stone, on the 26th November, the prosecution may show, if they can, that the witness is in error on both points; that the letter was revoked; that the contract was executed by his consent, and as what passed on this subject passed in writing, the Judge Advocate offers the letters as proof to that 120
end. The letters are the best evidence of their own contents; but the Judge Advocate has not objected to the witness stating his own opinions of their meaning and effect.

And the court, being closed, decided to admit the letter in evidence to the point stated.

The court was then opened and the decision announced, and the letter was then read as follows:

FORT MONROE, Dec. 6th, 1850.

J. R. ANDERSON, Esq'r, Richmond: 121

My Dear Sir,—I have your letter of the 2d instant. Dr. Carmichael called on me with a letter from General Talcott authorizing me to order of him a supply of shot and shells as I might require. Dr. C. it seems had some claim for an unfinished order on Wellford's foundry, and so far from telling either Gen. Talcott or myself that he had no interest in a foundry, but intended to sell the order in market, he *expressly stated* that he desired to get such an order to re-establish the foundry near Fredericksburg, in which he was formerly engaged, and which he said was to be managed by the son of Mr. Wellford, the former proprietor. 122

Knowing that he could only do the work *there* very slowly, I gave him the whole amount required that he might make preparations accordingly, not that he should deliver the whole quantity

stated at once, for I did not want them immediately, and have no
123 means of paying for them.

General Talcott received a letter from Mr. Kemble some time since saying that Dr. C. had offered the order to him, and that he (Mr. K.) had replied to him and agreed *to take it* provided the department consented to the transfer. Dr. C. did not wait for this consent, but at once sold the order to you.

On consulting with General T. we thought that, under the circumstances, we should decline consenting to the transfer of the order and I wrote to Mr. K. accordingly, but before any answer could be received from him, I was informed by Captain Stone that Dr. C. had transferred his order to you, and asking my in-
124 structions concerning it. I could only reply as I had to Mr. Kemble, refusing my consent to the transfer. I met Captain Walbach in Washington, at that time on his way to Richmond, and requested him to make an explanation of the matter to you; but, as you informed me, you were absent that week, he must have missed seeing you.

I was authorized by General T. to give the order, but am not provided with funds to pay for the articles, and he is not at all satisfied with Dr. Carmichael's proceedings, as it might have given him much trouble. As it is, I am glad it has fallen into the hands of a friend, for as the order does not contain the understanding we had with Dr. C. it is a plain one; and what I want
125 you to do, is to keep quiet about it and have a private understanding with General T. before doing anything in the matter. I have marked two words in the power of attorney sent, and which I return herewith, which are necessary to make it comply with the order; tho' this is of no consequence if we understand each other.

Very truly, yours,

BENJ. HUGER.

The Judge Advocate said that he offered that letter only as part of the correspondence which showed the part execution of
126 the contract with witness—and by his consent—and he now offered the whole correspondence.

And here, at 3 o'clock, the court adjourned to meet to-morrow at 10.

Thursday, 10 o'clock, 26th June, 1851.

The court met pursuant to adjournment. Present, all the members, the Judge Advocate and General Talcott.

The proceedings of yesterday were read over; whereupon, in
127 consequence of the temporary indisposition of one of the members, the court took a recess of fifteen minutes, at the expiration whereof the court again in session. Present, all the members, General Talcott and the Judge Advocate.

Colonel Benjamin Huger, a witness for the prosecution in continuation.

Judge Advocate—I proceed to offer in evidence to the point 128
stated yesterday, the correspondence in regard to the contract, and the execution of it, which passed between the witness and Anderson. The letters of Col. Huger offered appear to be originals, and will be exhibited to the witness to be identified. Of Anderson's part of the correspondence, the evidence is in part of the originals, and in part of copies. They will be likewise exhibited to witness that he may testify to the originals, and to the correctness of the copies.

This last by consent.

The Judge Advocate added, the first letter in the correspond- 129
ence read yesterday was of date the 6th December, 1850, I now offer a letter from Anderson to witness, dated 10th December, here exhibited.

Q. Is this letter here shown you the original letter from Anderson to you, dated Dec. 10th, 1850, and is it the next in order in the correspondence. *A.* Yes.

The letter then read as follows—

(*Private.*)

RICHMOND, Dec. 10th, 1850.

My dear Col.—Your letter of 6th inst. was duly received and I 130
am very much astonished to learn that Dr. C. has stated what he did to you and the General, about the place at which the shot were to be made.

I beg that you will allow me to make you acquainted with some circumstances, a simple narrative of which without any comment, will, I trust, fully justify my course in obtaining the control of the order and without waiting to communicate with you which I desired to do.

I was aware that Dr. C. had a claim on the Government for
a large contract for shot and shells, for he had brought the papers 131
to me several months ago, and solicited me to unite with him in
presenting and prosecuting this claim, proposing that I should be
equally interested in it. I unconditionally declined the proposition, being unwilling to connect myself or establishment with a
claim for a contract which I believed to have been improperly
promised. Still it appeared to me the faith of the Government
had been pledged and I thought it quite likely that a succeeding
administration, seeing the importance of preserving the credit of
the Government intact would direct the contract to be given to 132
him. His rights too were sustained by high legal authority.
Upon my declining his proposition, Dr. C. asked me if I would be
willing if he succeeded, to have the work done for him at the
Tredegar Works. I replied unhesitatingly that I would. He said,
that it would aid him very much, and asked me to put it writing,
which I did, and gave him the paper.

When in Washington a few weeks ago, I met a friend who told
me that Dr. Charmichael had succeeded in getting his contract
133 and that he mentioned it to me because he was aware that I was
to have the work done.

I returned home, and a day or two afterwards Dr. C. called at
my office, handed me your order and said he had but a few minutes
to remain, that he had several offers for it, one of which he
showed me, and that unless I agreed upon terms at once he would
go to the North the next day to sell his contract.

I had reason to believe that he had represented to the department
that I was to make the shot and if not, I believed that you
would be glad to have the order in the hands of a friend instead
134 of being hawked about to every blast furnace in the country, and
above all, I felt naturally very desirous to have the work for
my establishment, and I granted him such terms as were satisfactory
to him and made him an advance much heavier than I would
under other circumstances have made, as I had known him long,
and his family well, and knew how greatly in want of funds he
was, necessary to enable him to get to New Orleans.

Now knowing me I hope well enough to feel that you lose nothing
at least by the order being executed by myself instead of
Dr. C., I hope you will not hesitate to grant me every facility, and
135 I am certainly desirous of consulting your own convenience as to
funds. I would like to deliver some 10 or 15,000 shot as soon as
made, and I will afterwards confer with you as to the delivery of
the others. Please write me, say if I shall, and send me a pair of
32 pdr. guages.

Yours, truly,

J. R. ANDERSON.

P. S. As to the words of the power of attorney, I endeavored
to make it agree with the order, I have the order among my
papers however, and no doubt you have a copy of it which will be
136 all that is necessary for your guidance. As the power of attorney
makes *no transfer*, but is merely a matter between the principal
and agent, designed to show you that the power to sign his name
is delegated to me as agent, it appears to me that the terms of it
are not essential, except so far as they designate the order under
which I am acting. I put the papers in this form, believing it
would be more agreeable to you than a proposition to transfer
the order or contract on your books. Officially or otherwise you
are not aware of any transfer or sale of the contract, and therefore
you may, to me as you did to Mr. Kemble, decline to assent
137 to a transfer, but I do not ask for a transfer. I deliver the shot
in the *name of Dr. Carmichael*, and settle for him in *his name*,
just in this way I filled an order Mr. Tucker had from the Bureau
of Ordnance, and I hope this will satisfy you. Please drop me a
line by return mail as to delivery of 10 or 15,000 shot and
gagues.

Yours, J. R. ANDERSON.

Q. Is this your answer, to the letter just read? *A.* Yes, the letter here exhibited to witness now read as follows.

Fort Monroe, Dec. 18, 1850. 138

My dear Sir,—I have duly received your letter of the 10th inst. I do not suppose there will be any difficulty about the order for shot, I was only desirous on Gen. T's account to keep it quiet, and as far as you are personally concerned, shall be very glad if you can gain something by it.

I wish you would have an understanding with Gen. T. by writing either to Maynadier or to himself.

I will want a good many shells and sphre case shot, and after you get under way and your hand in, will send you an account of 139
them. Our small guage has been somewhat encreased in diameter, as you will see, Ordnance Manual, page 27. I will have a set arranged as soon as possible. I was absent at Balt. for a few days and did not get your letter until my return.

With best regards,
Yours, Truly,
BENJ. HUGER.

Q. Are these letters here shown you, letters from you to Anderson, and are they the next in order in the correspondence. *A.* They are my letters and I think they are the next in 140
order.

The letters shewn witness, then read as follows:

Fort Monroe, Jan. 4th, 1851.

Dear Sir,—Please send me on account Ordnance Department, 300 pounds $\frac{3}{4}$ inch round iron.

Respectfully yours,
BENJ. HUGER.

I am fitting out Capt. Stone's command for California. He expects a ship from New York daily, and he is to be off as soon as 141
his supplies can be got on board, and I can not stop a lathe to turn the guages. I have written to Maj. Mordecai to ask for a set to be sent to you, and issued to me when you have done with them.

I am glad to see Dr. A. looking so well. B. H.

Fort Monroe Arsenal,
January 11*th*, 1851.

Dear Sir,—Please furnish for Ordnance Department, 42 (forty-two) pieces rolled iron, ed., $2\frac{1}{2}$ feet long. $2\frac{1}{4}$—$1\frac{1}{4}$
Yours, BENJ. HUGER. 142

J. R. Anderson, Esq.

Q. Are these letters here shown you, true copies of the letters from Anderson to you, and are they the next in order of the correspondence? *A.* They are correct copies, and I think come next in order.

The letters of Anderson, dated January 18th and 1st Feb., 1851, here read as follows:

143 RICHMOND, January 18th, 1851.

COL. B. HUGER, *U. S. Army, Fort Monroe.*

Dear Sir,—I have received from Maj. Mordecai a pair of ring guages for 32 pdr. shot. I have the iron last ordered on hand $2\frac{1}{4}$—$1\frac{1}{4}$, but would prefer not sending it, as I could not recommend its quality for important purposes. It will yet be a couple of weeks before the works are in operation, when I can make it.

Yours, &c.,

(Signed) J. R. ANDERSON.

RICHMOND, Feb. 1st., 1851.

144 Dear Sir,—You will receive per schooner "Farmer," 3,100 32 pdr. shot, on account of your order to Dr. Carmichael. I will be pleased to have your opinion of them when inspected; and as to paying for them, suit your own convenience; we'll not have any difficulty on that score.

The captain was anxious to get his freight money at Old Point, but I had no authority from you to say he could get it, so you will use your pleasure about that.

I am yours, respectfully and truly,

145 (Signed) J. R. ANDERSON.

Col. BENJ. HUGER, *Old Point.*

This vessel engaged to take guns to Maj. Martin, for you, but went without them.

I never had as much difficulty before to ship cannon to Old Point, but I will send them the first opportunity.

(Signed) J. R. ANDERSON.

True copy.

BENJ. HUGER, *Bt. Col.*

Q. Is this your original letter to Anderson, and next in order?

146 *A.* It is my original letter, and comes, I think, next in order.

The letter here shown witness read as follows:

FORT MONROE,
Feb. 10*th*, 1851.

J. R. ANDERSON, ESQ.,

Dear Sir,—I find I have no cylinder guage for 32 pdr; will you have one made and forwarded to me by first opportunity. This guage has the same diameter as the large guage; it is made of cast iron, and is 5 calibres long. You have no doubt made them,
147 so there is no necessity of sending you a drawing.

The 32 pdr. shot sent, arrived on Saturday. I will require hereafter, the following spherical case shot, instead of *shot.*

2,000 32 pdr. spherical case shot.
2,000 24 " " "
3,000 12 " " "
1,000 6 " " "

The dimensions of guages (the new small guage is a little enlarged), and all the dimensions are given in the Ordnance Manual.
Where it is also stated, "spherical case shot must be made with 148
peculiar care, of the best quality of iron, in order that they may
not be liable to break in the gun." To which I may add that the
thickness at the bottom, should never be less than the *true* thickness, as this is the point which receives the shock of the balls.
Please send the cylinder guage for 32 pdr. as soon as you can
have it made.

Very respectfully and truly, yours,

BENJ. HUGER.

The shot have not been examined at all as yet; but I see the
seams show very plainly at the juncture of the flasks as if they 149
did not fit well.

Q. Is this a true copy of a letter from Anderson to you, and is it the next in order of the correspondence? *A.* Yes, I think so.

The letters of Anderson to witness, dated Feb. 17th, 1851, was read in evidence:

RICHMOND, *Feb. 17th*, 1851.

COL. B. HUGER, *U. S. Ordnance, Fort Monroe:*

Dear sir,—Your letter of 10th inst. was duly received and contents noted. I will proceed to make the projectiles ordered
therein. I will send you the cylinder guage for 32 pdr. shot by 150
the "Curtis Peck" of to-morrow. The appearance of a seam on
the shot must arise, I suppose, from some almost imperceptible
wear of the brass pattern. The flasks are all made of iron and
of the most modern and improved form, and as they fit tight, I
am satisfied it does not proceed from them. Before making any
more I will try new patterns, although the eye can not discern a
defect in the patterns which one would think could cause the apparent ring; I say apparent, because it is more perceptible to the
eye than to measurement.

There are but a few more that I will send down with Maj. 151
Martin's cannon.

Yours, &c.

J. R. ANDERSON.

Q. Is this your letter to Anderson, and next in order of time? *A.* Yes, it is my letter, and I think next in order of time.

The letter of Col. Huger to Anderson, dated Feb. 19th, 1851, here read in evidence as follows:

FORT MONROE ARSENAL,
Feb'y 19th, 1851.

Dear sir,—I have guaged and examined the shot sent by you.

Several of them have cavities or small holes the depth of which 152
exceeds 0.2 of an inch, the limit allowed by the regulations.

Nearly all pass the proper guage. A few would not go through the large guage on one diameter. The calibre guage you sent me

appears to have been used a good deal, and is in one diameter
153 0.02 too large.

12 have been rejected for cavities; they extend quite a depth under the surface. 3 too large for the proper guage, and *not being round.* Total 15.

I will send you a mem. of the number received as soon as they are piled. They are a fair lot of shot compared with others, but I hope practice will still make the moulders more perfect. I should like to have those iron bars now as soon as possible.

Very respectfully, yours,

BENJ. HUGER.

154 I leave to-morrow on a visit of a few weeks to Charleston.

Q. Is this letter a true copy of a letter from Anderson to witness, and does it come next in order in the correspondence? *A.* I believe it is a correct letter, but I was absent when it was received, and did not see it till my return from leave of absence towards the middle of April.

Letter here read as follows:

RICHMOND, *Feb. 28th,* '51.

COL. B. HUGER, *Commanding U. S. Arsenal, Old Point Comfort:*

Dear sir,—I hand you bill lading for 2000 shot. On the receipt
155 of your last, I caused a new cylinder guage to be commenced, which I will send you when finished, and the other can be returned. I was not aware that it was at all worn, and sent it, as it required some little time to make a new one.

I had the patterns for the spherical case shot to make which I have been getting up. I have just started my rolling mill, and will make the iron for you next week and forward it, finding you have not obtained it elsewhere.

Very respectfully, yours,

(Signed,) J. R. ANDERSON.

156 And the court adjourned to meet to-morrow at 10 o'clock.

---

10 o'clock, Friday, June 27th, 1851.

The court met pursuant to adjournment. Present all the members, Judge Advocate and Gen. Talcott.

The proceedings of yesterday were read over.

Col. Benj. Huger, a witness on the part of the prosecution.

Direct examination continued:

Q. Is this a true copy of a letter from Anderson to you, en-
157 closing the power of attorney; is it the first letter in the series of this correspondence, and is this a true copy of the power of attorney therein enclosed? *A.* Yes; this is a true copy of the letter. I think the original letter was presented to the court day before yesterday. This is a true copy of the power of attorney.

The letter and power of attorney here read as follows:

RICHMOND, *Nov. 20th*, 1850. 158

COL. B. HUGER, *U. S. Army, Old Point:*

Dear sir,—I enclose a power of attorney from Dr. E. H. Carmichael to attend to his order for shot, &c. Be good enough to place it on file, and to send me the necessary 32 pdr. guages.

Very respectfully, yours,

(Signed,) J. R. ANDERSON.

Know all men by these presents, that I, Edward H. Carmichael, of the city of Richmond, and the state of Virginia, do hereby constitute and appoint Joseph R. Anderson of said city, my true and
lawful attorney for me, and in my name and behalf to receive and 159
receipt for any and all payments due or that may be due me, for deliveries of shot or shell under an order from Benj. Huger, Brevet Colonel, Fort Monroe Arsenal, for 500 tons 32 pdr. shot, and such other quantity shot and shell not exceeding 500 tons, as the department may order, dated 8th November, 1850, hereby as fully confirming and ratifying all the acts of my said attorney in the premises, as if done by me in person; and I hereby agree and stipulate that this power shall in no wise be revoked without the written consent of said Anderson, my attorney.

In testimony whereof, I have hereunto affixed my hand and 160
seal this 18th day of November, 1850.

(Signed,) EDWARD H. CARMICHAEL.

Witness,

(Signed,) JOHN F. TANNER.

Q. So far as you know and believe, are the letters which have been exhibited to the court the entire correspondence between yourself and the proprietor of the Tredegar Works, Mr. Anderson, on the subject of your order to Carmichael? *A.* I believe they are the entire correspondence; they were considered unofficial by me, and no record was kept of them.

Q. Did you see Mr. Anderson during the period covered by 161
the correspondence? *A.* No.

Q. After your return to Old Point, in November, 1850, did you receive any further instructions from Gen. Talcott in regard to your order to Carmichael, or any instructions revoking the authority in regard to estimates and deliveries conveyed to you in his, Gen. Talcott's, letter of the 6th Nov., 1850. *A.* I received none whatever on the subject from Gen. Talcott, until a letter from him dated 11th April.

The defence asked now for the letter of the 11th April. The
Judge Advocate said he did not propose to put it before the court, 162
until, in the due course of the investigation, he had come to the events of the 11th April. But at the request of the defence, he now offered the letter.

It was read as follows:

163 ORDNANCE DEPARTMENT,
Washington, April 11th, 1851.

BREVET COL. HUGER, *Fort Monroe Arsenal.*

Sir,—You are requested to furnish this department all the information in your possession concerning any contract, order or arrangement of any kind, with Mr. J. R. Anderson, to furnish for himself, or any other person, shot or shells for Fort Monroe, or the arsenal.

Please report the character of such arrangement, (copy of agreement or order,) what articles have been called for under it,
164 and what deliveries made, with any remarks or explanations on the subject that you may deem proper.

Respectfully your ob't serv't,
(Signed) G. TALCOTT,
Bt. Brig'r Gen., Col. of Ordnance.

Q. Were you present at any conversation between Carmichael and Gen. Talcott, and do you *know* anything that Carmichael said to the General? *A.* I never saw them together during any part of this business.

Q. Had Anderson any contract with you, or any order from
165 you, for 32 pdr. shot, other than the order to Carmichael. *A.* None.

The direct examination of this witness rested here for the present.

Cross examinatian—

Q. Had you any communication, direct or indirect, official or otherwise, with Gen. Talcott, touching the order to Carmichael, or the transfer to Anderson, after the refusal to recognize the transfer to Anderson in Nov., 1850, until you were ordered by Gen. Talcott to report to him upon that subject in April last?
166 *A.* None whatever.

Q. Have you here a copy of the report made by you in pursuance of that order; if you have, produce it? *A.* I have not a copy, and did not bring one as the original is on file here in the ordnance office.

Original here handed to defence by Judge Advocate for their examination, with the remark that the prosecution would offer it when it was reached in the order of time.

Q. Did you at any time, and when, report to him that any attempt had been made to carry the order to Carmichael into ef-
167 fect by the delivery of shot or otherwise? *A.* I made no report to him whatever on that subject, till my reply to his letter of the 11th April, calling for a report.

Q. Had you any further or other authority from Gen. Talcott in reference to the procuring of the shot and shells, than the order of the 6th Nov., recited in the charges? *A.* No sir.

Q. Did you ever make any estimates of funds required for

payment for the shot sent to Fort Monroe by Mr. Anderson? *A.* None.

Re-examined by Judge Advocate— 168

Q. You say, on the cross examination and in answer to the question next before the last, that you had no further authority from General Talcott in reference to the procuring of shot and shells than the order of the 6th November. Do you mean that you received no authority from him personally here in November 1850? *A.* None, unless his approval of my letter to Anderson by Stone, and my letter to Kemble, be considered as such, which I do not.

No further examination of this witness at present by the pros- 169
ecution or defence.

The court was here closed, and, after deliberation, again opened. Present, the accused.

Col. Huger a witness.

Q. by the court. In the correspondence between the witness and Mr. Anderson, which has been read, about shot and shells, did the witness consider Mr. Anderson as making these shot and shells on account of the order to Dr. Carmichael or on his own (Anderson's) account, or on any other account? *A.* I considered him as making them at his own risk, under the order transferred
to him by Carmichael, and expected he would get the consent of 170
the department.

Q. by the court. In one of your letters to Mr. A. you speak of the inspection of certain shot delivered by him, and also of the reception of shot. You, in another letter, order some shrapnell shells for him. Were these things connected with, or in execution of the order of General Talcott in favor of Dr. Carmichael? If not, under what authority were they said or done? *A.* There was no official inspection of the shot. They were inspected by me in compliance with a request from Mr. Anderson contained in one of his letters. Directions for an official inspection are contained in the regulations of the Ordnance Department in
articles 116, 117, 118. 171

The articles referred to by witness read here as follows:

The inspection and proof of ordnance and projectiles, shall be made, under the direction of the Colonel of Ordnance, by such officers of the Ordnance Department as the Secretary of War may, from time to time, designate for that purpose; who will be held strictly responsible that all ordnance and projectiles received by them for the United States, shall have been subjected to the inspection and proof required, and that they shall conform, in all respects, to the established models.

The inspecting officer of ordnance and projectiles at the foundries, shall give to the contractors triplicate certificates of inspection 172
according to form No. 32.

Duplicate reports of inspection of ordnance and projectiles at the foundries (forms 33 and 34,) shall be made immediately after

each inspection, one copy to be forwarded to the Chief of the Ordnance Department; and in the month of October, a consolidated report (form 35) of all such inspections made during the
173 year ending 30th September, shall be forwarded by the inspecting officer to the Chief of the Ordnance Department. The inspecting officer will keep books in which shall be recorded all reports which he is required to make, and all correspondence connected with this particular service. These books will be carefully preserved, and in case of relief, turned over to his successor.

Col. Huger, a witness:

Q. by the court. Did the witness ever, directly or indirectly, make known the fact, to the Ordnance Bureau or its Chief, or to
174 the War Department, that said Anderson was employed in making shot and shells as set forth in the correspondence? *A.* No.

Q. by the court. Was the freight for the delivery of said shot and shells, as set forth in the correspondence which has been read, paid for? If so, by whom and on what account? *A.* The bills of lading made them payable by the shipper. For the convenience of the captain I did pay the freight on account of Mr. Anderson, and not on account of the United States.

Q. by the court. Under the general instructions of General Talcott of November 6th, 1850, to procure the shot and shells by open purchase, how came the order to be given to Carmichael.
175 *A.* Because *he* brought it to me was one reason, and I expected them to be made at a foundry near Fredericksburg, from which I had formerly received both shot and shells of very good quality.

Re-examined by Judge Advocate upon the examination by court, by permission of court.

Q. You state in your answer to the court, that you considered Anderson as sending the shot at his own risk, and that you expected him to procure the consent of the department. Did you say anything on this point to Anderson other than is found in the letters before the court. *A.* Nothing.

176 Witness said, I desire to make an explanation under permission of the court, and to say that I considered the correspondence with Mr. Anderson private, as I had already given him my official answer by Captain Stone, and as it commenced in an argument on his part to convince me that he had a right to deliver the shot under the power of attorney, in which I thought he was in the right; but I expected him to procure the consent of the department, and which I thought would be granted, because I could see no detriment to the United States in so doing.

Q. by Judge Advocate. As your letters to Mr. Anderson before the court are not marked private, and were on official business,
177 do you consider he was warned that you regarded them as private? *A.* He received no warning. My letters are not marked private, but his first and second letter was so marked.

The Judge Advocate then said to witness—I am directed to
bring to your attention the question heretofore put by the court,
and to ask an answer to that part of it which refers to shrapnell 178
shells, or spherical case shot.

A. The letter ordering them states, that they are to be furnished instead of shot, and it was my intention to have them furnished under that order to Carmichael, and at the rates therein specified, otherwise they would cost a much higher price. None were furnished. I received, in the month of April, an order from the Secretary of War to receive no supplies of shot or shells from any founder or manufacturer, a copy of which I enclosed to Mr. Anderson.

Joseph R. Anderson, a witness for the prosecution, sworn in
due form of law. 179

Examination in chief, by Judge Advocate.

Q. Did you send any 32 pdr. shot in this year to Col. Huger for the United States? If so, under what authority did you send them? *A.* I did make two shipments under the authority of an order to Dr. Carmichael from Col. Huger, assigned to me by Dr. Carmichael. I also held a power of attorney from Dr. Carmichael to deliver the shot, to which I have referred in his name.

Q. How many did you deliver? *A.* I don't remember the exact number delivered. I think between five and six thousand.

Q. What objections were made, if any, by Colonel Huger to 180
receiving shot from you under that order. *A.* The objection I
believe, was in a letter from Captain Stone. It is contained in
this letter of 26th November, from Captain Stone. (Captain
Stone's letter of that date, heretofore entered on this record at
page , here shown the witness.) I did not regard this objection as final.

Here the accused interposed the following objection :

The accused respectfully suggests that it can have no weight
or bearing upon the charges or specifications against him, to ascertain what was the construction put by the witness upon writ- 181
ten papers already before the court, and that even if any inference could be drawn from such construction, (which the accused does not perceive), the admission would not be justified by any precedent, so far as he is advised, in any court, civil or military.

The questions put by the court to Col. Huger, stands upon totally distinct ground, being in the nature of cross examination by the court, in order to reconcile supposed contradictions in the testimony of that witness.

G. TALCOTT,
Bt. Brig'r Gen., Col. of Ordnance. 182

The Judge Advocate said he had laid before the court the correspondence between Col. Huger and Mr. Anderson, to prove the

execution of the contract. The letters were the evidence of their own contents, and he had not thought it admissible to give Col.
183 Huger's construction of them. But as in answer to enquiries from the court, Col. Huger had put his own understanding of the letters in evidence, and the facts connected therewith, the Judge Advocate felt under a necessity to offer this testimony from the other party to the correspondence, the witness now under examination.

And the court being cleared, after due deliberation decided "that the objections be overruled, and the witness proceed."

The court was then opened, and the decision announced.

The witness, Joseph R. Anderson, continued his testimony on
184 his direct examination as follows:

I did not regard this objection as final, because Capt. Stone states (I read the words from his letter) that he, Col. Huger, thinks Dr. Carmichael had, *under the circumstances*, no right to transfer his order for shot without first consulting him, and obtaining his consent; and I regarded the subsequent letters of Col. Huger as giving his consent.

Q. When, if ever, did you receive orders to stop the work? *A.* I received notice from Col. Huger in writing, (I have it not here,) some time subsequent to the 12th April, of this year, of
185 orders received by him directing him to receive no more shot; I will add, that previously to my receiving this letter from Col. Huger, I heard the Secretary of War give such orders to Gen. Talcott; this happend in my presence, and I think on the 12th April.

Q. Did you at any time while you were executing, as you supposed, the order of Col. Huger to Carmichael, notify Gen. Talcott thereof? *A.* I did not.

Q. Do you mean to say that you never have to this day? *A.* I received a letter from Gen. Talcott, dated, I think, the 10*th*
186 *April*, 1851, making enquiries of me; I answered that I never notified him before.

Q. What amount, if any, did you give Carmichael for the privilege of executing his contract, as assignee and attorney? *A.* Six thousand five hundred dollars, $6,500·00; I paid him that.

Q. Are you the proprietor of the Tredegar Iron Works in Richmond? *A.* I am.

On reading over his testimony to witness for correction, he said "I wish to add to that part of one of my answers which states that I considered Col. Huger's letters subsequent to the
187 letter of Capt. Stone dated 26th Nov., 1850, as giving his consent, and say that I considered his letters and acts as giving that consent.

Questions by Judge Advocate:

Q. Had Dr. Carmichael any foundry or any interest in any foundry when he obtained the order from Col. Huger? *A.* None that I know of.

Q. Had you ever any conversation with Gen. Talcott on that
subject? *A.* I never had prior to the 12th April, when I called
in person to answer his letter, of the 10th April, which I had re- 188
ceived as I was passing through Washington.

And here the hour of 3 having arrived, the court adjourned to meet tomorrow at 10.

---

10 o'clock, Saturday 28th June, 1851.

The court met pursuant to adjournment. Present, all the members, Judge Advocate, and Gen. Talcott.

The proceedings of yesterday were read over. Morris Adler,
a witness on the part of the prosecution being sworn in due form 189
of law, testified as follows:

Q. Are you a clerk in the Ordnance Office of the War Department, if yes, how long have you been so? *A.* Yes and I have been since the year 1832.

Q. Say whether or not you furnished Dr. Carmichael with a
list of the prices paid by the Ordnance Bureau for shot, and if you
did, state what passed between you and Gen. Talcott on that
matter, if any thing, and give the time as near as you can. *A.*
I gave the prices. It was my own act on the same morning I
acquainted Gen. Talcott with the fact, to which he made no ob- 190
jection. I think it was on the 7th of November, 1850.

Q. At that day, the 7th November was the letter from Gen. Talcott to Col. Huger, dated the 6th November, 1850, in regard to open purchases of shot at Fort Monroe recorded in the office, and did you know of it? *A.* Dr. Carmichael presented to me the order when he asked me for the prices.

Q. Did you give the lowest prices? *A.* I thought I had, I
gave the prices rather hurriedly to Dr. Carmichael; the same day
I think, I looked over the book, and discovered, an account of
shot procured from Savary and Co. of Philadelphia, who had fur- 191
nished some at $2\frac{3}{5}$ cents per pound. I felt much mortified at this
oversight, and I immediately informed Gen. Talcott of it. He
expressed great displeasure at this oversight of mine and censured
me a good deal for having furnished the prices at all in the first
instance. I asked the General what I should do about it. He said
nothing. I then stated to Gen. Talcott that I would write a
private note to Col. Huger, to which he made no objection, and I
wrote the note.

Q. At what hour of the day did furnish the memorandum to
Carmichael, and at what hour did you first inform Gen. Tal- 192
cott thereof? *A.* It must have been between 8 and 9 in the
morning that I gave the memorandum; before office hours, I informed Gen. Talcott directly after he came to the office, which was about his usual hour of coming, about 9 or a little after,

Q. Do you know the hour at which the cars leave here for

Baltimore. The first train after 8? *A.* I never go to Baltimore, I did not then know the hour, except what Dr. Carmichael told me.

193 No cross-examination by defence.

Capt. Wm. Maynadier, U, S. Ordnance Department, a witness on the part of the prosecution recalled.

Examination in chief, resumed—

Q. You stated when previously before the court, that you returned on the 11th November to the Ordnance Office (from which you had been for a time absent,) state now, when thereafter, you first, if ever, had any conversation with Gen. Talcott on the subject of any contract given to Carmichael, for shot, and state all that passed between you and the General on that subject? *A.*
194 When I went to the Ordnance Office on the 11th November, 1850, I mentioned to Gen. Talcott the substance of a conversation I had just had with a gentleman on the street, which was that the gentleman asked if it was true that Dr. Carmichael had got a big contract for shot from the Ordnance Department; that he had heard such was the case; and that Dr. Carmichael had offered it for sale to a founder in Baltimore, that I had informed the gentleman that I had been absent from the office, since the middle of Oct. and knew nothing about, but that I would examine the books at the office, and let him know if it was so.

Gen. Talcott told me that he knew nothing about the contract
195 referred to in the conversation; and that all that had been done in the relation to the purchase of shot during my absence would be found in his letter to Huger of the 6th November, which was on record; I read that letter as copied on the books.

Q. Were you informed by the Gen'l that the letter had been sent to Huger by Carmichael? *A.* I was not; either that it had or had not been so sent.

Q. When, if ever, and what was the next communication between yourself and Gen'l Talcott in regard to an alleged contract with Carmichael for shot? *A.* To the best of my recollection, the next communication between us, on that subject, was about
196 the end of December, 1850, when I read a letter to him from Mr. Anderson, who enclosed to me therein a copy of the order of the 8th November, from Huger to Carmichael, which is on your record. It was a private letter, in reply to one which I had written to Mr. Anderson, answering one he had previously written to me sometime after the middle of December, and in which he enquired whether I knew, whether there was anything personal to him in the objection which Huger seemed to have to his executing the order to Carmichael. This letter I have not preserved. My answer was that I knew nothing of the facts of the case, and
197 could give no opinion on it; that I did not even know what Huger's order to Carmichael was, as I had never seen it.

Q. When you read as you say, to Gen'l Talcott, Anderson's letter, did you read him also, the enclosed copy of the order from

Col. Huger to Dr. Carmichael? *A.* I showed it to him; I don't think I read it to him.

Q. Did the Gen'l make any explanation or remark to you on 198
the subject of the order to Carmichael? *A.* He made none.

Q. Will you read to the court the 132d article of the regulations for the government of the Ordnance Department? *A.* The 132d article of the ordnance regulations reads as follows:

No contract for the service of the Ordnance Department, shall be made by any officer or agent thereof, except by special authority from the chief of the Ordnance Department, sanctioned by the Secretary of War; and all officers or agents making contracts shall strictly observe the provisions of the laws on that subject.
(See appendix No. 2.) Contracts shall be made in triplicate, one 199
of which shall be forwarded to the chief of the Ordnance Department, at the date of the contract, that it may be deposited in the office of the second comptroller within ninety days thereafter, as the law directs.

Q. Will you read the *provisions of laws* which the article just read refers to? *A.* The article refers to appendix No. 2, which read as follows:

APPENDIX No. 2.

Extracts from laws relating to contracts. 200

Article 1st. All purchases and contracts for supplies or services for the military service of the United States, shall be made by or under the direction of the chief officer of the Department of War.

2. From and after the passage of this act, no member of Congress shall, directly or indirectly, himself or by any other person whatsoever in trust for him, or for his use or benefit, or on his account, undertake, execute, hold or enjoy, in the whole or in part, any contract or agreement hereafter to be made or entered into with any officer of the United States, in their behalf, or with any person authorized to make contracts on the part of the
United States. 201

3. Nothing contained in the preceding article shall extend, or be construed to extend, to any contract or agreement, made, or entered into, or accepted, by any incorporated company, where such contract or agreement shall be made for the general benefit of such incorporation or company; nor to the purchase or sale of bills of exchange, or other property, by any member of Congress, where the same shall be ready for delivery, and for which payment shall be made at the time of making or entering into the contract or agreement.

4. In every such contract or agreement, to be made, or en- 202
tered into, or accepted, as aforesaid, there shall be inserted an express condition that no member of Congress shall be admitted to any share or part of such contract or agreement, or to any benefit to arise thereupon.

5. All purchases and contracts for supplies or services which
are, or may, according to law, be made by, or under the direction
203 of, either the Secretary of the Treasury, the Secretary of War,
or the Secretary of the Navy, shall be made either by open purchase or by previously advertising for proposals respecting the same; and an annual statement of all such contracts and purchases, and also of the expenditure of the moneys appropriated for the contingent expenses of the military establishment, for the contingent expenses of the navy of the United States, and for the discharge of miscellaneous claims, not otherwise provided for, and paid at the treasury, shall be laid before Congress at the beginning of each year, by the secretary of the proper department.

6. No contract shall be made by the Secretary of State, or of
204 the Treasury, or of the Department of War, or of the Navy, except under a law authorizing the same, or under an appropriation adequate to its fulfilment.

7. No advance of public money shall be made in any case whatever: but in all cases of contracts for the performance of any service, or the delivery of articles of any description, for the use of the United States, payment shall not exceed the value of the service rendered, or of the articles delivered previously to such payment; provided, that it shall be lawful, under the special
direction of the President of the United States, to make such
205 advances to the disbursing officers of the government, as may be necessary to the faithful and prompt discharge of their respective duties, and to the fulfilment of the public engagements.

Q. Those are all the provisions of law referred to in that article, to wit, 132d article of the ordnance regulations? *A.* Those are all.

Q. Will you read to the court the articles on the subject of contracts which follow the 132d article, or any others which bear upon that subject? *A.* The only other articles bearing on that subject which follow the 132d article read as follows:

206 133. The rights vested in a contractor, for services to be performed, or supplies to be furnished for the Ordnance Department, shall, in no case, be transferred to any other person or persons; but such contractor shall be held to his legal responsibilities, and all payments shall be made to him only.

134. Payments on account of any contract to the amount of four-fifths of the value of work done, or of services performed in part, may be made, in case the contract embraces operations of long continuance. Such payments on account, under an unfulfilled
contract, not being admitted at the treasury, will not be charged
207 in the quarterly accounts; but a statement of all such, specifying the amount of each, will be annexed to the duplicate account current, which is designed for the files of the ordnance office, in order that the true state of the funds on hand may be known.

Witness continued—

There is another article on this subject which precedes those I

have read, being the article *No.* 8 of the Ordnance Regulations; it
reads as follows:

8. Ordnance and ordnance stores shall be provided by open 208
purchase, by fabrication or by contract, as may be most advantageous to the public service. They shall be provided by ordnance officers only, except when otherwise specially directed by
the chief of the Ordnance Department, or in cases of urgent necessity; and in such cases a report and certificate showing the
necessity, from the officer ordering the purchase, will be required
for the admission of the account of purchase at the treasury.

The Judge Advocate said he would interrupt the witness, to
put before the court the letter which witness had received from
Anderson, and which he read to Gen. Talcott, as heretofore 209
stated in his testimony.

The letter here read as follows:

(*Private.*)

RICHMOND, Dec. 26th, 1850.

My Dear Maynadier,—Your esteemed favor of the 24th, is received, and as I wish you to know the exact facts, I enclose a
copy of Huger's order to C.

Now, when it is remembered that C. applied to me to unite
with him as a partner in his application for these shot, which I
declined, as I was unwilling to be his partner, and that I did give 210
him, at his solicitation, a written promise to make the shot at
the "Tredegar Iron Works," if *his* claim should be allowed, and
that he asked for the writing that he might show the department
that he had the means of complying with his engagement, you
will not think it strange that I supposed H. and the General
knew when they gave him the order that I was to make the
shot, and when I took up the order which he was hawking about,
I supposed, and am certain still, if they knew the facts they
would thank me. And for this reason, if no other, that they knew
I would say to them, I will consult your own convenience 211
about the time of executing this order. Now, when C. brought
the order to my office, he made another proposal of partnership
in the manufacture of the shot, which I declined for reasons
that may be well understood by those who know Dr. C. well.
He was about going to New Orleans with his family to live, and
asked me a very large sum, which I gave him, for the unconditional transfer of the order; I have not thought proper to state
this officially or otherwise, to Col. H., because I also took from
Dr. C. a power of attorney to deliver and settle for shot *in his*
name, thinking that might be more agreeable to him, and per- 212
haps he and the General might prefer not to know that Dr. C.
had sold his contract; I know you will not communicate it if
best not to do it; but you peceive, with Dr. C. I could not be
safe unless I took in the order.

I am yours, truly,

J. R. ANDERSON.

Q. How many contracts for cannon and projectiles have, since
you have been connected with the Ordnance Bureau, been exe-
213 cuted in the written form directed by the 132d article which you
have read. *A*. I remember but one; that was a contract made
on previously invited proposals for furnishing certain heavy
cannon, while Mr. Wilkins was Secretary of War; I have examined the records, and find none other made in that form.

Q. What form and mode of making such contracts has been
followed in all other cases, or generally? *A*. The form has generally been, to give an order to a founder directing him to make
for the Ordnance Department a certain number of cannon or
projectiles. That has been the general rule; the formal written
214 contract within in triplicate made by Mr. Secretary Wilkins, is
the exception. I say written in triplicate because, if the regulation was followed, it was so written; but I am not sure that it
was. I can examine the books, however, if it be material, and see.

Q. You say the form of making these contracts has been by
giving orders to founders. Have these orders been in writing,
and by what officer given? *A*. They have been in writing, and
given by the chief at the Ordnance Department.

Q. Is there any established form of language in which these
orders have deen expressed? *A*. The orders sometimes bear on
215 their face the evidence of having been given by direction of the
Secretary of War, by stating such to be the case. But more frequently they bear no such evidence, and appear to emanate from
the Chief of the Ordnance Department.

Q. Have you knowledge of particular instances wherein the
order does not state that it is given by direction of the Secretary
of War, and was yet, in point of fact, given in pursuance of his
instructions; or are you able to state generally how this fact has
been in such cases? *A*. I have no knowledge on that subject.
I never questioned the authority of the Colonel of Ordnance, or
where he got his authority.

216 *Q*. Is it the usage in the Ordnance Department, in ordinary
speech and in letters and reports to the War Department, to style
these engagements between the government and the founders,
contracts? *A*. We sometimes call them contracts and sometimes
orders, and are not particular about the distinction of those
terms.

Q. Does the bureau make a consolidated report to the War
Department, of contracts and purchases, annually, and is such
report sent to Congress with the Executive message? *A*. The
bureau makes annually, to the Secretary of War, a statement of
all contracts made, and a separate statement of open purchases.
These statements are made to be laid before Congress in compli-
217 ance of 5th sec. of the act 3d March, 1809.

Q. Under which head, in these reports or statements, are these
orders to founders entered? *A*. Under the head of "open purchases" always.

Q. How are your small arms designated in reference to the fabrication? *A.* As national armory, and as contract arms.

Q. How are these last procured? *A.* From private manufacto- 218
ries. Formerly they were generally on written contracts according to the forms prescribed by law and regulations; but sometimes on extensions of those contracts by written orders; latterly, I think they have been procured more generally on such orders.

After examination of the record book the witness added: In the years ending December 1846, 1847, 1848 and 1849, these contracts, arms were procured entirely on written orders, and are reported among the open purchases.

Q. Did the Secretary of War call on the Ordnance Department,
on the 21st January of this year, for a statement of all contracts 219
chargeable upon certain appropriations? *A.* He did.

Q. Did you answer the call? *A.* I prepared the answer from the records of the Ordnance office and took it to General Talcott, who was temporarily confined to his quarters by indisposition.

Q. In this report to the Secretary, in answer to his enquiries about contracts, did you report as contracts, and style contracts, engagements contracted by these written orders? *A.* I did. No other species of contracts constituting charges upon those appropriations then existed to my knowledge. At the suggestion of
the general, for more complete explanation to the secretary, I 220
added a note specifying the articles and quantities to be delivered under the orders. The particular phraseology of the note is my own.

The Judge Advocate said he had exhibited the papers to the witness to enable him to put exactly in evidence the words of the papers about contracts; the papers themselves belong to another part of the case, and therefore are not now offered for the record.

The defence had no objection.

Q. Have you an abstract showing all the contracts and open 221
purchases from Wellford's foundry. *A.* I have none with me.

The Judge Advocate said that he must have that information before the court.

The Judge Advocate proposed to suspend the direct examination of this witness and call another witness who had applied for his discharge, to which proposal the court assented.

Joseph R. Anderson, a witness recalled by prosecution. Direct examination resumed by Judge Advocate.

Q. Who paid freight on the 32 pdr. shot you sent to Old Point 222
Comfort? *A.* It was paid by the commanding officer of the arsenal.

Q. Have you refunded it to him, or authorized it to be charged to your account? *A.* I have not refunded it, and Colonel Huger, in the customary quarterly settlement which has since taken place, has not charged me with this freight; I mean the public account between the United States and my establishment for iron, shells for experiments, and such other articles as the Fort Monroe Arsenal procure from me.

223 *Q*. Has he given you notice of any such charge against you on your private account? *A*. None. I have no private account with Colonel Huger.

Q. Where did Dr. Carmichael live of late years, and what his occupation, and what his pecuniary resposibility? *A*. He has lived in Richmond of late years, is a physician, and I think is generally regarded as insolvent.

And here the court adjourned to meet on Monday, the 30th instant, at 10 o'clock.

---

224 Monday, 10 o'clock, June 30th, 1851.

The court met pursuant to adjournment. Present, all the members, the Judge Advocate and General Talcott.

The President of the court stated that General Walback's health did not permit him to continue to sit as a member of the court; that the General had been laboring under a serious indisposition for several days, with no prospect of a speedy convalescense, and that he thought the General ought to be excused from the court.

General Walback stated that he was quite sick, but if it should
225 be the pleasure of the court, he would endeavor to sit.

The prosecution and defence were desirous that General Walback should remain if his health would permit, but desired to leave it to be decided by himself and the court.

Whereupon, by consent of the court, General Walbeck retired and vacated his seat.

The proceedings of yesterday were read over.

Captain William Maynadier, a witness for the prosecution, in contiuation.

Direct examination—

Q. You have read to the court from 133d article of the Ord-
226 nance Regulations, that the rights of contractors shall not be
transfered; that each contractor shall be held to his legal responsibilities, and all payments shall be made to him only; will you state to the court now, whether, according to the established usage of the Ordnance Bureau, and of the Treasury, payments on contracts, as well as on all other accounts, are not made to attorneys on power of attorney, duly authenticated, and also to heirs and legal representatives? *A*. A payment to a regularly constituted attorney, on proper powers of attorney, in the Ordnance Office and in the Treasury, is regarded as a payment to the
227 person himself, and in like manner to heirs and legal representatives, on due evidence.

Q. Are projectiles for cannon ever found by government ready made and for sale in the market, or have they ever been procured except when made to order? *A.* Never to my knowledge.

Q. You have said that supplies are procured by the Ordnance
Bureau on written orders, and that these engagements by the
usage of the bureau are designated as "*contracts*," and as *open*
"*purchases*;" will you now say what distinction, if any, between
"contracts" and "open purchases" according to the usage of 228
your bureau, is conveyed by an order to procure shot by "open
purchase only?" *A.* I understand such an order to prohibit the
making of a formal written contract, but as authorizing an order
to be given to supply the shot at discretion as to the *person*.

Q. Describe the process of making payment to a contractor
where the contract or open purchase is made directly with the
Ordnance Bureau? *A.* The inspecting officer of the articles
procured, sends to the ordnance office certificates of inspection,
setting forth the articles inspected and received; to that certifi- 229
cate is appended evidence of the receipt of the articles by some
officer or agent of the Ordnance Department, also the account of
the person furnishing the supplies; these papers are examined in
the ordnance office, and are then transmitted to the second Auditor
of the Treasury, with a statement endorsed that the within account has been examined, and so much is found due therein to a
certain person, to be paid from such an appropriation; then
the Ordnance Department is done with it; it then becomes a
treasury matter; and then, after examination by the auditor, it
is sent to the the second comptroller for further examination; 230
the comptroller returns it approved for so much, and the auditor
sends it to the Secretary of War in order that he may draw on
the Treasury Department a requisition for its payment.

Q. Describe how the payment would be made in case of a
formal written contract under seal, and made by an officer commanding at an arsenal, and what notice of such payment would
be furnished to the Secretary of War in the ordinary course of
office? *A.* The contract itself would be sent to the Ordnance
Bureau, and submitted to the Secretary of War for his approval
before being filed in the second comptroller's office; payments 231
under the contract would be made by the disbursing officer of the
arsenal, on ordinary vouchers, which would accompany his next
account current; that account current would be examined in the
ordnance office and transmitted to the second Auditor of the
Treasury for settlement, with a letter from the chief the Ordnance Department informing the auditor whether he approved or
disapproved of all or any particular part of it.

Q. Now inform the court how payment would be made under
"an open purchase" made by an officer commanding an arsenal,
and what notice of such payment would be furnished to the Sec- 232
retary of War in the ordinary course of office? *A.* Payment
would be made by the disbursing officer of the arsenal, on ordinary vouchers, which would reach the ordnance office with his
next account current, and go through the same process of exami-

nation and transmittal to the second auditor as stated in the previous answer; no notice to the Secretary of War of such pay-
233 ment would be furnished that I know of; the Secretary of War has the power to call for all accounts of officers of the army in the Treasury Department.

Q. Is such examination of the accounts of disbursing officers, after they have passed into the Treasury Department made by the Secretary of War in the ordinary course of office, or have you ever known it to be done? *A.* It is not ordinarily made, and I have never known it to be done.

Q. Say if you know of any mode according to the course of your office, and the settlement of accounts there, by which a large
234 amount of shot could be procured and paid for and not be brought *directly* to the knowledge of the Secretary of War, except by an "open purchase" made by a disbursing officer at an arsenal? *A.* Even by the last mode it could not escape being reported to the Secretary, (in the annual report of the operations of the Department made before each session of Congress;) that so many shot, or other articles, had been procured during the preceding fiscal year by fabrication of purchase. If the articles had been paid for through the Ordnance Office, such payments would appear on the annual statement of articles procured by open purchase, or
235 contract, as the case might be; but they would not appear on that statement if paid for by the disbursing officer of the arsenal. When paid for through the bureau, the statement would show that they had been procured by contract or purchased. When paid for by the arsenal, the Secretary would not distinguish from the reports what articles were procured by fabrication and what by purchase. They would be lumped together.

Q. Does your office, make an annual report to the Secretary of War showing *in detail* the articles procured by purchase or contract during the year. If so, state how that report is made?
236 *A.* The office makes annually in January, a statement of contracts made during the year ending the previous December; and a separate statement of articles obtained by open purchase or ordered during the same year.

The first statement specifies names of contractors, articles contracted for, the price to be paid, the place of delivery, the date of the contract, and by whom made.

The other statement specifies from whom purchased or ordered, the articles purchased or ordered, the place of delivery, the price paid or to be paid, and the date of the order.

237 *Q.* Are these statements confined to the articles procured by the bureau, or do they include the purchases made my disbursing officers at the arsenals? *A.* They do not include the purchases made by disbursing officers at the arsenals, but are confined to those made by, or paid through the bureau.

Q. Have you ever known a founder offering to enter into contracts to furnish projectiles for cannon, referred by the bureau to

the officer commanding an arsenal, or have you known such contracts or purchases made otherwise than by the bureau? *A.* I do not recollect ever to have known a founder so referred. In
some instances when an officer *at an arsenal* wants a supply of 238
shot to fill an order for supplies, or to enable him to carry on the operations of his arsenal, he has ordered them direcly from a founder and paid for them himself.

Q. Have contracts for amall quantities of projectiles been made directly by the bureau? *A.* Not for small quantities. I should call anything over ten tons a large quantity. That is my opinion merely. All quantities of projectiles for cannon, exceeding those required to fill orders for supplies, or for some special purpose at an arsenal, have been ordered by the Ordnance Bureau.

Q. Have you ever known so large a contract for projectiles as 239
one for 500 tons given at any one time to one establishment? *A.* I have never known so large an amount ordered at one time from any founder. I will, however, add that during the Mexican war, when we were fitting out the expedition for Vera Cruz, unlimited orders for shells were given to many founders; that is to say, they were authorized to make as many as they could make by a given time.

Q. Does your office, in issuing orders to an officer of ordnance, directing an inspection at a foundry, set out in the order, that
the Secretary of War appoints him an inspecting officer for that 240
purpose? *A.* It does not generally; it may sometimes.

Q. When was the last work done by the foundry of Wellford, near Fredericksburg, for your department? *A.* The last delivery of projectiles was *in April,* 1847; I don't know when the work was done.

Q. Is there any information in your office in regard to the suspension of operations by that foundry, after the death of Mr. John S. Wellford? *A.* There is no information there that I know of in regard to the suspension of operations; there is information
showing the death of Mr. Wellford; I do not recollect the time. 241

Q. Will you examine this paper; say if is a copy of a report from your office to the War Department? *A.* I believe it to be a true copy.

Q. Can you say what change in the state of the appropriations referred to in that report, or the supply of cannon balls in the possession of the Ordnance Department, had taken place between the date of this report, 8th January, 1851, and the 1st November, 1850, exclusive of the contract with Carmichal? *A.* No material change that I am aware of.

The Judge Advocate here offered the copy of the report, 242
which copy had been exhibited to the witness, with the question preceding the last, and said to the defence that he had received this copy from the War Department, where he had been informed

that the original report had been sent to Mr. Calvin. The defence required no further proof, and admitted the copy.

The report was here read as follows:

243 ORDNANCE DEPARTMENT,
Washington, January 8, 1851.

HON. C. M. CONRAD, *Secretary of War:*

Sir—In answer to Mr. Samuel Calvin's letter of this date,
referred to this office, I have to report, that our present supply of
cannon balls, in proportion to that of cannon and gun carriages,
is such as to render it unadvisable to enter into a contract for a
further supply of balls. The amount of available funds which
can be legitimately applied to this object, is now quite limited.
The prices which have been paid for cannon balls, have varied,
244 according to the state of the iron market, from two cents to three
and a quarter cents per pound. Now that iron is unusually low,
I suppose that they could be procured at the cheapest rate.

Mr. Calvin's letter is returned herewith.

Respectfully your ob't servt.,
(Signed.) G. TALCOTT,
Bt. Brig. Genl. Colonel of Ordnance.

Cross-examination by defence.

Q. If Col. Huger had received, on public account, the shot and
shells delivered by Anderson, would not the regular and necessary
245 course to pay for them have required him to forward to the
Ordnance Bureau estimates specifying the quantities and prices
of the shot and shells? and would it not have been necessary to
have the Secretary of War's requisition, specifying the appropriation,
before the money could be drawn from the treasury necessary
to pay for them? *A.* It would have been necessary for Col.
Huger to have forwarded an estimate to the Ordnance Department,
stating what funds he required, for what purpose, and from
what appropriation; and he could not have got the money without
a previous requisition from the Ordnance Department on the
246 Secretary of War, stating in gross the amount to be remitted, and
the appropriation under which Col. Huger was to be held accountable
for the same.

Q. If the amount required was unusual, or if for any other reason the Secretary desired to enquire into the particulars, would not the records of the Ordnance Department, in such a case, plainly lay open to him the facts and particulars? *A.* They would plainly lay open every fact and every particular.

Q. Please examine the printed congressional document now
shown to you, and purporting to be a copy of the Report of the
247 Colonel of Ordnance Department, of the 4th November last, and
say whether it does not contain purchases made, not by the Bureau,
but by the disbursing officers of the arsenal. *A.* It does
contain such purchases, among which I notice particularly 27,054
cubic feet of timber, among the articles reported as procured by

purchase and fabrication at the arsenal, and in the report of the
commander of the Watertown Arsenal, which accompanies the
report of the Colonel of Ordnance, it is stated that 276 spherical
case shot were inspected at contract establishments. It would 248
not follow necessarily that these spherical case shot were purchased by the commander of the arsenal. This officer is a contract inspector, and reports among his year's work the inspections
he has made.

Q. If the order for shot and shells by Colonel Huger had been
sanctioned by the Ordnance Department, and the order executed,
would not the annual report of that department to the War Department, under the head of articles procured by purchase and
fabrication, have necessarily shown that they were purchased
and not fabricated? *A.* It would have shown that the shot had
been procured by purchase or fabrication, and as the department 249
does not fabricate shot, it would necessarily have followed that
they were purchased.

Brevet Major Alfred Mordecai, a witness on the part of the prosecution, being sworn in due form of law, testified as follows:

Direct examination, by Judge Advocate.

Q. Did you send any 32 pdr. shot guages to Mr. Anderson in
January of this year? and if so, did you communicate the fact
to the Colonel of Ordnance and procure an order for doing so?
A. I did send two 32 pdr. shot guages to Mr. Anderson in January of this year. I sent them at the request of Colonel Huger, 250
conveyed to me in an unofficial letter; and to the best of my
recollection, before sending them, being at the ordnance office, I
mentioned to General Talcott that I had received such a letter
from Colonel Huger, and that I presumed there would be no objection to sending the guages to Mr. Anderson, and I think that
he replied, "No, I suppose not," or something of that kind. I
will add that, attaching very little importance to the transaction,
my recollection of the conversation with General Talcott on the
subject is not very positive. I received no written authority, I
know, for the issue of these guages to Mr. Anderson; such issues
are generally made only on written orders from the Colonel of 251
Ordnance. These guages were issued to Mr. Anderson, but they
were receipted for by Colonel Huger, to whom Mr. Anderson was
told that they would be turned over when he was done with
them, and consequently, in the statement of work done in the
month of January, which was made to the Ordnance office early
in February, (on the 3d I think,) the guages are reported as having been issued to Colonel Huger, and that is the only official
report on the subject made by me to the Colonel of Ordnance.

Defence suggested to witness to state the date of the conver- 252
sation with General Talcott.

To which he said, I can only fix it by reference to certain papers, after examining which, witness said, "It must have been between the 8th and 10th of January.

Cross examination, by defence.

253 *Q.* Was there any thing in the request of Colonel Huger, or in what you said to General Talcott, inconsistent with the supposition that the guages were required for making a few shot for experiments? *A.* On the contrary, that was my impression at the time that they were required for that purpose, and for that reason I attached so little importance to the matter.

And then the court adjourned to meet to-morrow, the 1st July, at 10 o'clock.

---

254 10 o'clock, Tuesday, July 1st, 1851.

The court met pursuant to adjournment. Present, all the members, Judge Advocate and General Talcott.

The proceedings of yesterday were read over.

Thomas B. Barton, a witness on the part of the prosecution, being sworn in due form of law, testified as follows:

Direct examination, by Judge Advocate.

Q. Will you state to the court where you reside, and your means of being acquainted with the partnership affairs of Well-
255 ford & Co., the proprietors of a foundry near Fredericksburg, Virginia? *A.* I reside in the town of Fredericksburg, Virginia; was the counsel of William N. Wellford, executor of John S. Wellford, who was the principal owner and partner of the Catharine Furnace company. In June, 1847, I was called upon by the executor, and by Messrs. Carmichael and Deane, (the two last owning $\frac{1}{5}$th each of the property of the company in the furnace,) to settle their transactions.

Q. Will you state whether that foundry is in operation? if not, when it ceased? *A.* It is not, and ceased, to the best of my
256 memory, between March and June, 1847, and has not been in operation since. In fact the parties endeavored to sell it, and there was a contract of sale, but the purchaser did not comply with the terms, and the property stands in the same hands; but Carmichael's interest is covered by deeds of trust to secure Wellford and other creditors far exceeding its value.

Q. Had Dr. Carmichael, to your knowledge, any other foundry, or any interest in any other foundry? *A.* Not to my knowledge.

Q. What was his *general reputation* for pecuniary solvency? *A.* He was not considered as solvent or in good circumstances.

257 *Cross examination*, by defence.

Q. Do you mean to be understood as saying that Doctor Carmichael's interest in the establishment has not been disposed of by him, otherwise than by the execution of two deeds of trust by way of mortgage to secure certain debts, and that those deeds of trust have not been enforced by sale under them? *A.* Yes sir, I do mean that.

Q. Do you recollect the date of the first of those deeds of 258
trust? *A.* I do not, I think it was in 1845, or perhaps before it.

Q. Was there any assignment, or deed of trust, or mortgage, upon the other shares or either of them? *A.* Francis B. Deane, had given a deed of trust on his share.

Captain William Maynadier, a witness for prosecution recalled.

The Judge Advocate said he had recalled the witness at this
time, only to prove a paper; that this paper had only become
known to him, and as he understood to the department, on yesterday; otherwise he should have made it known to the defence,
with the other documentay proofs, which he had exhibited to 259
them before the trial. He would further state, that Col. Huger
had also given him some information in regard to this letter on
yesterday morning.

Q. Whose writing is this? *A.* This paper is in the hand-writing of Col. Huger. I never saw it, never knew that it was on the files of the Ordnance Office, and never knew of its existance until yesterday morning.

The paper exhibited to the witness here read as follows, *by the witness.*

(Unofficial.) 260

FORT MONROE ARSENAL,
Nov. 5th, 1850.

GENL. G. TALCOTT.

My dear Genl.—Dr. Carmichael has handed me your note of the 1st Nov.

The number of 32 pdr. guns intended to be mounted at this
place is about 187. As it is probable that 8 in. Columbiads or
Howitzers may be substituted for some of them we may suppose
about 150 32 pdrs. would be mounted here, which for service 261
should be provided with shot, at 500 rounds each, this would require 62,000, from which deduct the number on hand 28,450,
leaves 33,550, or nearly 500 tons. There is room to place these
shot here, and they are in convenient position to be transported
elsewhere of required. I would recommend not to procure any
42 pdr. shot as it is highly probable the 8 in. Columbiads will
take the place of 42 pdr. guns.

Very respectfully and truly, yours,
BENJ. HUGER.

Foregoing letter endorsed as follows: 262

C. B. HUGER,
FORT MONROE ARSENAL,
5th Nov. 1850.

States quantity of shot on hand and the additional quantity which could be stored at that port,

Received 6th Nov. 1850. *A.* 6th Nov.

Q. Look at the endorsements on that letter and say in whose
263 hand-writing they are? *A.* All the endorsements except the last are in the hand of Mr. Jonas B. Keller, the registering Clerk of the Ordnance Bureau.

The last endorsement is in the hand-writing of Gen. Talcott.

Q. Does your office mode of making these endorsements show the date of the receipt of letters, and the date of the answer made to them. And does this letter show these dates? *A.* Yes, this letter shows in the hand-writing of the registering Clerk, that it was receieved on the 6th Nov. 1850, and in the hand-writing of Gen. Talcott, that it was answered 6th November.

264 *Q.* Does your record of letters show any answer to that letter? *A.* Our letter book shows but one letter dated 6th Nov. 1850, it is the letter on your record of that date, in regard to the purchase of shot.

Q. Where was this letter found, and where were you when it was received by your bureau? *A.* The letter was found in its regular place on the files of the office; I was absent from the bureau at the time it was received, as I have before stated.

Q. by defence. In your testimony heretofore given, you have read to the court certain regulations touching the purchase of
265 supplies; will you look at the paper now shown you, purporting to limit from or after its date, the discretion of the Colonel of Ordnance in making such purchases, and say whether it is a true copy of an order of the Secretary of War, and when it was promulgated? *A.* I believe this to be a true copy of the order received from the Secretary of War on the day of its date, or a day or two after.

The order was read as follows:

QUARTER MASTER GENERAL,
266 COMMISSARY GENERAL,
COLONEL OF ORDNANCE.

The Quarter Master General, the Commissary General, and the Colonel of Ordnance, will not hereafter make or authorize any contracts for supplies, or for arms and munitions of war, to be furnished, or for services to be performed, to an amount exeeding two thousand dollars, without previously submitting such contracts or propositions to the Secretary of War.

C. M. CONRAD,
Secretary of War.

267 WAR DEPARTMENT, January 29th, 1851.

C. M. Conrad, Secretary of War, a witness for the prosecution, recalled.

Direct examination by Judge Advocate:

Q. Will you relate to the court what enquiries you made of General Talcott in regard to any contract for shot, after or before the interviews between yourself and Dr. Carmichael, and

what answers you received; be pleased to relate all that occured?
A. Shortly after I took charge of the War Department, several applications were made to me by different persons for contracts 268
to make shot; these persons speaking for themselves, or in behalf of friends; among the first of those who applied, was Mr. Thomas Green, of this city, who spoke in behalf of some friend who owned a foundry in Virginia; I enquired of General Talcott (verbally, of course, as these things are usually done in the department) whether the department would be in want of shot during the current fiscal year, which terminated yesterday; General Talcott told me that the department did not want shot; that there was an ample supply on hand; I accordingly communicated that answer to Mr. Green, and I think to one or two others, telling them, how- 269
ever, that at another time if the department should be making shot, I would give them all a chance of sharing in the profits; some time after this conversation with Mr. Green, he came to the department and reminded me of what I had told him, but told me that I was mistaken in what I had said, that the department was not making shot this year, for that he had learnt that the Tredegar Iron Works had a large contract for shot for the War Dopartment; I said it could not be so; but as he persisted that he could not be mistaken, I told him I would enquire into the subject, and let him know the result; on the same or 270
the next day, I sent for General Talcott, and informed him of what Mr Green had stated to me; he said that it was a mistake; that no contract existed for shot, and that none was making at Richmond for the department; I informed Mr. Green of this result of my enquiry, and supposing it was all a mistake, I dismissed the subject from my mind entirely; some time after this (I do not recollect the precise interval between the two visits), the same gentleman came again to the office and told me that he had positive information, of the truth of which he had no doubt, that a large quantity of shot was making at the Tredegar Works, in 271
Richmond, owned by Mr. J. R. Anderson, and that a considerable quantity was piled up in the foundry yard, or some where about the foundry; I endeavored to persuade him that it was a mistake, but as he seemed incredulous, I told him that I would have a written report upon the subject, which I would exhibit to him, and he would see that he was in error; I accordingly directed a note to Gen. Talcott; it was some time in January. A paper here exhibited to witness by Judge Advocate, on which he stated:

This note of the 20th January, 1851, is the note I allude to.

The paper here read as follows: 272

To the Colonel of Ordnance:

The Secretary of War requests a statement of the expenditures made from the appropriations of the 28th of September last, for "armament of fortifications, and ordnance, ordnance stores and supplies," and of existing contracts chargeable upon those appropriations.

War Department, *January* 20, 1851.

273 Witness resumed: To which I received the following answer. The answer here read as follows:

Ordnance Department,
Washington, January 22d, 1851.

Hon. C. M. Conrad, *Sec'y of War:*

Sir,—I respectfully submit herewith, the statement requested in the note from the War Department, dated 21st inst. It may be proper to remark farther in regard to the appropriations referred to, that the balances on hand 28th September, 1850, were
274 sufficient to meet expenditures up to that time, and no *deficiency* was created. It is supposed that the balances now remaining, or the greater part of them, will be required during the present fiscal year for the current operations of the arsenals, repairs, preservation and addition to the armaments of forts, purchase of gun carriage timber and of supplies for the troops and posts.

Respectfully, your ob't serv't,

(By order.) W. MAYNADIER,
Capt. of Ordnance.

275 In the foregoing letter was enclosed the following statement:

Statement of expenditures from the appropriations for "armament of fortifications, and ordnance, ordnance stores and supplies," since the last appropriations on the 28th September, 1850, and of existing contracts chargeable upon these appropriations.

	Armaments of Fortifications.	Ordnance, Ordnance Stores, and Supplies.
276 Expended since 28th September, 1850,.....	$26,378·62	$54,416·76
Amount of contracts chargeable,..........	31,417·00*	21,230·00†
	$57,795	$75,646·76

(By order.) W. MAYNADIER,
Capt. of Ordnance.

Ordnance Department, *Jan. 22d,* 1851.

Witness resumed:

I then asked for more explicit information, and this memoran-
277 dum was sent up.

* Sixty-five 32-pounder iron cannon, ordered and to be delivered, $31,417.

† Nine hundred and fifty officers' swords, eight 32-pounder bronze howitzers, and spare parts for repairs of carbines and pistols, ordered and to be delivered, $21,230.

The memorandum exhibited by witness then read as follows:

Amount of money due on ordnance and ordnance remaining to be delivered under existing engagements under the appropriations for "armament of fortifications," and "ordnance, ordnance stores 278
and supplies," viz:

Armament of Fortifications.

Alger, 30 32 pdr. guns,	$14,600
Freeman, Knapp & Totten, 30 32 pdr.	14,600
G. Kemble,	2,217
	$31,417

Ordnance and Ordnance Stores.

Ames, 950 officers' swords,	$14,250	279
" 8 32 pdr. bronze howitzers,	6,100	
	$20,350	
North, carbine parts,	401	
Aston, pistol "	479	
	$21,230	

Witness resumed:

As that statement did not mention for what particular articles the sums mentioned had been paid, I sent down to the Ordnance 280
Bureau this note, dated the 23d January.

The note here read as follows:

To the Colonel of Ordnance:

The Secretary of War requests that the principal items be stated, making up the sums of $26,378·62, from "armament of fortifications," and $54,416·76, from "ordnance, ordnance stores, &c.," expended since the 30th of September last, and the names of persons to whom the principal payments were made.

WAR DEPARTMENT, *Jan'y 23d*, 1851. 281

Witness resumed:

In answer to which this statement was sent to me.

The statement here read as follows:

ORDNANCE DEPARTMENT,
Washington, January 23d, 1851.

Hon. C. M. CONRAD, *Secretary of War:*

Sir,—In answer to the note from the War Department of this date, I have to state that the expenditures from the appropriations 282
for "armament of fortifications," and "ordnance, ordnance stores and supplies," since the 30th September last, were for the following items, viz:

For the current service of the arsenals. consisting of wages to hired men employed in making gun carriages, purchases of iron, timber, paints, and other materials required for the manufacture
283 of gun carriages, implements and equipments for forts, and repairing carriages, &c., mounted thereat—paid to various persons in small sums:

Armaments of Forts.

	$11,773·26
Paid Joseph R. Anderson, proprietor of the Tredegar Iron Works, Richmond, Virginia, for 30 32 pounder iron guns,	14,605·36
Total,	$26,378·62

284 For the current service of the arsenals, consisting of wages to hired men employed in the manufacture of siege and field carriages, implements and equipments, and the purchase of materials for making these carriages, implements, equipments, and harness; of accoutrements for the troops and repairing arms, carriages, &c.; of materials for, and the preparation of field and siege ammunition, and for altering flint lock muskets to percussion—paid to various persons in small sums:

Ordnance, Ordnance Stores and Supplies.

At fifteen arsenals and two armories,	$49,937·04
285 To C. Alger & Co., of Boston, for 24 12-pounder bronze mountain howitzers,	3,982·12
To L. North, of Middletown, Conn., for parts for repairs of carbines,	401·80
To H. Aston, of Middletown, Conn., for parts for repairs of pistols,	95·80
Total,	$54,416·76

Respectfully, your ob't serv't,
286 G. TALCOTT,
Bt. Brig. Gen'l, Col. of Ordnance.

The witness continued:

As the words, paid to various persons, in small sums, at fifteen arsenals and two armories, were used in connection with the large sum of $49,937, &c., I determined to make a more direct enquiry in relation to shot, and accordingly sent to the Ordnance Bureau, on the 27th January, the note of which this is a copy.

The paper exhibited by witness here read as follows:

287 The Secretary of War requests to be informed what contracts have been made for *shot* from the last appropriations; how much has been furnished and how much yet to be furnished, and whether any further contracts are contemplated.

WAR OFFICE, *January 27th,* 1851.

To which I received this answer. The paper here exhibited by witness read as follows:

ORDNANCE DEPARTMENT,
Washington, January 27th, 1851.

HON. C. M. CONRAD, *Secretary of War:*

Sir,—In answer to the note from the War Department of this
date, I have to report, that no contract has been made for shot by 288
this department, from the last appropriations; no shot have been
furnished. There are no contracts for shot made by this department unfulfiled, and none are now contemplated.

Supposing that the inquiry may have reference to a letter officially addressed to Bt. Col. Huger, on the 6th November, 1850, I deem it not improper to send you a copy of that letter, although not specifically called for by your note. Col. Huger's estimate for the present quarter, the only one received from him since the above date, contains nothing for the purchase of shot.

Respectfully your ob't serv't, 289

G. TALCOTT,
Bt. Brig. Genl., Col. of Ordnance.

(Copy.)

ORDNANCE DEPARTMENT,
Washington, 6th November, 1850.

COL. B. HUGER, *Fort Monroe Arsenal:*

Sir,—It may be well to provide more shot and shells from time
to time for the post of Fort Monroe, and for this purpose you are 290
authorized to procure them to a reasonable extent if, as I suppose, (the price of iron being now so low) they can be had on favorable terms. You will make the necessary estimates of funds to meet the deliveries as they occur; they should be procured by open purchase only.

I am, Sir, respectfully, your ob't serv't,

G. TALCOTT,
Bt. Brig. Genl., Col. of Ordnance,

NOTE.—Since the above was written, a quantity of shot has
been taken from Fort Monroe for the supply of guns sent to Cal- 291
ifornia, the vessel being laden at that fort. Supplies for the more southern forts are also frequently sent from Fort Monroe.

Witness continued—This answer being perfectly satisfactory, I ceased to think on the subject until my attention was again called to it a short time after, by Mr. Green again mentioning that shot were making at the works at Richmond, when it occurred to me that possibly Col. Huger might be making shot under that order of the 6th November. I either sent for General Talcott, or he came
on other business to my office, I forget which, when I mentioned
this subject to him, and asked him what was meant by that order, 292
whether it might not be construed to authorize the making of shot, and what he meant by it. He told me no, that could not be so;

that all the shot that could be needed at the Monroe Arsenal were occasionally a few shot or shells for artillery practice and experiments; that sometimes a shot or shell, of a description of which there was none on hand, was required in their experiments and
293 practice, and that the object of this letter was to authorize the commander of the arsenal to purchase them as they were needed; that it was possible Col. Huger might have ordered something of this kind, but that it must of course be a very inconsiderable quantity.

The next interview that I recollect having on this subject, was a very considerable time after the last conversation, when Mr. Green came again to the office, about the 3d or 4th of April, and informed me that a large quantity of shot had actually been sent down to the Monroe Arsenal from the Tredegar Works, in
294 Richmond. He asserted this so positively, and stated that he had received the information from a person who spoke from personal knowledge, and of whose veracity he could entertain no doubt whatever; that I began to suspect that there must be some mistake in this matter, and I told Mr. Green to make a statement in writing, and that I was determined to investigate the matter fully. He told me he would do so, and a day or two afterwards he sent me this letter. Several days intervened after I received the letter, before I could deliver it to General Talcott. I think a Sunday intervened, and one day, I think he was attending the funeral
295 of a naval officer, at all events several days elapsed, when I sent for him to come to the office. I commenced by reminding him of our previous conversations on the subject of these shot that were said to be making at the Tredegar Iron Works in Richmond, and asked him whether he had heard any thing more on that subject since we last conversed on it. He said he had not. I told him "I have received a letter from Mr. Green, a few days ago, which I would beg leave to read to you." I read to him Mr. Green's letter from beginning to end. The letter here read as follows:

296 WASHINGTON, 5th April, 1851.

HON. C. M. CONRAD, *Secretary of War.*

Sir,—During the last summer and autumn, I presented the application of my friend, Mr. F. B. Deane, of Lynchburgh, Va., to make shot and shell for your department; Mr. Deane had executed such work to the satisfaction of your predecessor, and also of the Navy Department; the reports to the latter will that his work has been done as well as at any foundry in the Union. He has done more to develop and establish the iron interests of Va., than any man in it. But the convulsions of 1837–8 and 9,
297 overwhelmed him so far as to force the sacrifice of his heavy interests in the great Tredegar Iron Works at Richmond, and his successors reaped the profits which his genius had foreseen when he planned and built up the establishment. Crushed almost, but not subdued by adversity, his energy and the confidence of

his friends enabled him to establish a new foundry at Lynchburgh, in the vicinity of the best iron ore of the state. The
departments gave him work to do, the profits of which were all 298
applied in settlement, without discount or composition, of his old
debts. But for some reason wholly unknown to him, the en-
couraging countenance of the War Department was divested
from him, without the least complaint as to the execution of the
work, while his opulent rival owning the Tredegar Works (which
he had erected and been compelled to sacrifice), has directly and
indirectly had almost constant employment for that department,
as I am informed. Mr Deane's time not being constantly occupied in doing the work for the Navy Department, he undertook
a new enterprise, which seemed almost chimerical, and subjected 299
him to the ridicule of some of his friends; the building of the
Virginia and Tennessee Railroad. Like Peter the hermit, he
went through the long tier of southwestern countries, and finally
awakened such an interest and exerted such influence in the
Legislature and among the people, as to overcome all obstacles,
and in one year after this, the whole line will probably be finished
from Lynchburg to Tennessee To Mr. Dean's energy, by common consent, the country is more indebted than to any dozen
others for this great work. Such a man, poor, intelligent, honorable and enterprising, ought to be sustained, when it can be 300
done fairly, quietly, and without injury to the public interests.

These views heretofore presented by Members of Congress,
who pressed his application upon you for work, induced you to
say he should have a fair proportion of such as the department
required. I beg leave most respectfully to suggest that fair proportion would be an amount equal to that which the Tredegar
Works (the rival in making shot and shell) has been authorized, since your kind promise was given, to execute for the
department. I do not say any contract has been made between
the department and Mr. Anderson of the Tredegar Works, since 301
your promise to us, but I am authorized to say, the Tredegar
Iron Works have been engaged, and are now engaged in executing a large amount of work for the delivery of shot and shell to
the department. Whatever authority for doing this work exists,
was probably given by the department or its officers to Dr. Ed. H.
Carmichael, recently a resident of Richmond, but now of the city
of New Orleans. During a recent visit to Richmond, I was informed the work was done by Mr. Anderson, under an assignment from Dr. Carmichael. I beg to be understood as making
no complaint at your department's giving the employment to Mr. 302
Anderson; I think it is right to give a large proportion, *if not
all* to southern foundries, for some years to come, as from the
foundation of the governmnnt such a vastly disproportionate
amount has been given to the north. But if you will pardon the
expression, I do say, after the promise made by the head of the
department, Mr. Deane has a just expectation of receiving an

order for a like amount of work as that which Mr. Anderson has
obtained. No matter who gave the order, the work is done *for*
302 *the government*, and a large amount of shot has recently been
delivered at Old Point Comfort by Mr. Anderson. If you will
direct an order to be given to Mr. Deane for a like amount of
shot and shell as that which is authorized by the order under
which Mr. Anderson is working, Mr. Deane will be satisfied, and
if the work is not as well done, he will abide the penalty.

I am yours, most respectfully,

THOMAS GREEN.

Witness resumed—When I had finished reading the letter, I
303 said to Genl. Talcott, "General, what do you say to that"? He
answered, I say that there is not a word of truth in it. It is all
a humbug from beginning to end; with great emphasis. He spoke
very emphatically, and apparently with some displeasure. I said to
him, General, there must be some mistake in the matter. People
cannot fancy that they see shot piled up in a foundry yard, or that
they see it laden on board a vessel, and they could have no motive
for fabricating such a story, and there must be some truth in it,
some foundation for it. He reiterated his assertion, that there
was no truth in it, that there was no foundation for it. I en-
304 deavored to create doubts in his mind and labored to show how
improbable it was that such things could be invented; that this
thing came direct from Richmond; that Mr. Green told me that
the person from whom he had the information, was a person of
undoubted respectability, and that he would be willing to testify
in the matter if necessary. He still insisted, however, that the
story was without foundation. I then said, "Then General, you
must make a report to me on this subject." He answered, "I
make my report now, what further report do you want? I told
him I wanted a formal report in writing. He said, with some
305 impatience. "If I was to make a dozen reports, I could only report what I now say, that there is not a word of truth in it. I
replied, nevertheless, General, I must have a report in writing
on this letter, at the same time, extending to him the letter which
I held in my hand. He said, I should have a report in writing,
and left the room. This was about the 10th of April. Two or three
days afterwards, he came to the office, accompanied by a gentleman, whom he introduced to me as Mr. Anderson of Richmond,
Virginia. He observed as soon as he entered, Mr. Anderson is
the owner of the Tredegar Works, and I have brought him to
306 you to explain that matter of the shot. I instantly replied,
General, I want no explanation on that subject from Mr. Anderson, whatever explanation is given must come from yourself.
He said that as Mr. Anderson was the gentleman who was making
the shot, and knew all about it, he thought he could best explain
it. I observed, then there is shot making. He answered, it
seems so. I answered, well then, General, I will receive no

explanations on that subject from any one but yourself. I have directed you to make a written report on that subject, and I will
accept no substitute for it. He said he did not offer it as a substi- 307
tute, but he thought I would like to hear Mr. Anderson's statement. I said Mr. Anderson could make his statement in writing, Mr. Anderson then spoke, and said it was hard he could not be heard on a subject in which he had a pecuniary interest; I replied that he had no interest in this question; that if he had any claim against the department, he had only to present it, and it would be considered and decided. But the present question was one between the head of the department, and one of its officers. It was a question whether an order of the department had been disobeyed, whether
or not false reports had been made to the department by one of 308
its officers; and that was a question which did not concern him. He said he had acted in good faith, had executed part of the work, and had made his preparations to execute the remainder, had delivered part of the shot, and that he should not suffer for the faults of others. I told him this was not the time for that enquiry, and refused to converse with him on the subject. In the course of conversation he mentioned that he had executed the work, under an order given by Col. Huger to Dr. Carmichael. Gen. Talcott left the room first, and as he was about to retire, I
said to him, "General you will please direct Col. Huger to receive 309
no more shot or shells. He answered, "it was hardly necessary, he took it for granted he would receive no more." I told him, General, you have taken too much for granted, already, in this matter. You took it for granted that no contract existed, when you were informed to the contrary; you took it for granted that no shot had been made; and that no shot had been delivered; when you were informed that there had been. Now I beg of you to take no more for granted, but to issue the order. He said he would do so, and left the room. This is as well as I can recollect
it, the purport of the conversation that took place. 310

Some five or six, or may be ten days afterwards, he made me his report.

Judge Advocate—Is this it?

Witness—Yes this is the report; the date is the 19th of April.

The report here exhibited to witness with its enclosures, read as follows:

Ordnance Department,
Washington, April 19th, 1851.

Hon. C. M. Conrad, *Secretary of War:*

Sir,—On the subject of Mr. Thomas Green's letter of the 5th 311
instant, referred by you to this office, I have to report, that the facts in regard to the work stated to be now under execution by Mr. J. R. Anderson, for this department, will be found explained in the enclosed copy of a letter from this office to Brevet Colonel Huger, dated 6th November, 1850, and the accompanying letters

from Brevet Colonel Huger and Mr. J. R. Anderson, dated 17th April. 1851.

312 My letter of the 6th November is the only authority given by me for procuring the shot and shells for this department; it contemplated, as it clearly expresses, the purchase in open market, to a reasonable extent, of such quantity of these articles as might be required for the post of Fort Monroe. Colonel Huger's letter states his reasons for giving the order dated November 8th, 1851, to Doctor Carmichael, which order, it appears, was not executed as the doctor had induced Colonel Huger to believe it would be, but was transferred to Mr. J. R. Anderson, as explained in the letter of that gentleman.

The quantity of shot and shells ordered by Colonel Huger, five hundred tons, is more than the department is, in my opinion, in
313 immediate want of; but as they will be required sooner or later, and are imperishable articles, no loss can result from providing them in anticipation of need for their actual use. With this supply I do not think it would be advisable, so far as regards the present wants of the service, to give any further orders for shot or shells, unless it may be to fill requisitions (should any be made) for such kinds and calibres as may not be on hand. It is not probable that any such requisitions will be made, although it is possible; but they can not require purchases save to a very limited extent.

314 Mr. Green's letter is returned herewith.

I have the honor to be, sir,

Your obedient servant,

GEN. TALCOTT,

Bt. Brig. and Col. of Ordnance.

Enclosed in the foregoing report, the two letters which here follow:

FORT MONROE ARSENAL,
April 17th, 1851.

315 BR. GEN'L GEO. TALCOTT, *Ordnance Department:*

Sir,—In reply to your letter of the 11th instant, I have to state that, on the receipt of your letter of the 6th November, '50, I gave to Dr. Edward Carmichael an order to furnish shot, &c., for this post, a copy of which order is herewith enclosed, dated 8th November, 1850. I should, perhaps, explain that Dr. Carmichael had been engaged with Mr. J. L. Wellford in supplying shot and shells from a foundry near Fredericksburg, Va., and they had furnished them of very good quality. The foundry was a small one I knew, and expected it would take several years to
316 complete the order, and they could be paid for on limited annual estimates. Dr. C. induced me to believe the work was to be done at that foundry. As the work was to be inspected here, I knew he would be compelled to execute it faithfully, and I con-

sidered the price reasonable, and it would be an advantageous arrangement for the department. The quantity would not give to guns required for this post alone one-half the number of 317
rounds required for each piece in service. (See Ordnance Manual, page 337.)

It seems Dr. Carmichael, did not execute the order at the foundry at which he induced me to believe he would, but transferred it to Mr. J. R. Anderson, of Richmond. Mr. Anderson has sent to this post an account of Dr. Carmichael, 5,070 32 pdr. shot.

I send also enclosed an order of mine to J. R. Anderson to furnish spherical case instead of shot, and an order from Major Laidley to him for some special shells for experiments. These 318
are all the orders that have been given to him.

I remain, very respectfully,
Your obedient servant,
BENJ. HUGER, *Bt. Colonel.*

NOTE.—In the foregoing report from General Talcott were also enclosed copies of his order of the 6th November, 1850, to Colonel Huger, and of Colonel Huger's order for shot to Dr. Carmichael dated the 8th November, both of which are heretofore recorded on this record, and therefore omitted here.

319

TREDEGAR IRON WORKS,
Richmond, April 17th, 1851.

GENERAL G. TALCOTT,
Ordnance Department, Washington City:

Sir,—Your letter of 10th was received in my absence. Some time in November last Dr. E. H. Carmichael called at my office and stated that he had agreed to furnish the War Department at Fort Monroe five hundred tons of 32 pdr. shot, with a conditional contract for five hundred tons more of shot and shells, and having made up his mind to remove to New Orleans, he wished to 320
get me to perform his contract for him.

We entered into an arrangement under which he gave me a power of attorney, which I forwarded to Colonel Huger, whose order he turned over to me, and a copy of which order has been furnished the department; and it may not be amiss to add that I advanced to the doctor as much as it was estimated he could realize from the work. I am not able to state how much of the work has been done. But I have contracted with moulders to do the whole and purchased the iron for it, and have probably completed about three-fifths of the quantity, or near it. 321

I have the honor to be,
Your most obedient servant,
J. R. ANDERSON.

The witness resumed—Not being satisfied with this report, I wrote to Colonel Huger to repair to Washington. He did so,

and came to the department. I conversed with him on the subject and reduced his statement to writing in his presence as it
322 was delivered, and he signed it. After taking Colonel Huger's statement in writing, I sent a copy of it to General Talcott, enclosed in a letter from myself to him, in which I called his attention to the various verbal and written reports which he had made to me on this subject, and which appeared to me at variance with his present report and with the statement of Colonel Huger, and requested that he would furnish any explanations, or additional testimony that he might consider necessary.

Judge Advocate—Is this his answer?

Witness—Yes, this is his report in answer to my letter.

Judge Advocate—I now offer the report of General Talcott to
323 which the witness testifies, and the letter from the War Department to which it is in answer, and read them in the order of their dates.

W. D., Washington, May 1, 1851.

Sir,—I have read with attention your report on the letter of Mr. Thomas Green, referred to you some time since.

Early last fall, (several applications having been made to me for orders to make shot and shells,) I sent for you and asked you whether the department needed a supply of those articles. These
324 inquiries you always answered in the negative.

Some time in January last I was informed that the proprietors of certain iron works in Richmond had, or were supposed to have, a contract with the department to make shot and shells. On my questioning you on this subject, you told me that it was an error; that no such contract existed. A few days afterwards you were directed to furnish a statement of the expenditures made from appropiations for the current year for "armament of fortifications," and for "ordnance, ordnance stores and supplies," and of "existing contracts chargeable upon these appropriations." This
325 statement was furnished. In your letter transmitting the same, dated January 27th, 1851, you state that "no contract has been made for shot by this department from the last appropriations; no shot have been furnished; there aré no contracts for shot made by this department unfulfilled, and none are now contemplated."

In the same letter you furnished the department with a copy of your letter of the 6th November to Col. Huger. In a conversation with you on the subject of this letter, you stated its object was to enable the commander of the arsenal, at Fort Monroe, to purchase shot and shells in small quantities as were required,
326 from time to time, for experiments and artillery practice.

At a later period, I think some time in February, or perhaps early in March, I was informed that a large quantity of shot were being made for this department at the Tredegar Works in Richmond, and that a portion had been already made and piled up at the foundry. I again informed you of what I had heard, and told

you that my information came from a source that left little room
to doubt of its correctness. I am not sure, indeed, that I did not
mention the name of the person who had communicated this in- 327
telligence to me, to wit, Mr. Thomas Green of this city. You
assured me, however, that there was not the slightest foundation
for the story, and although the circumstance struck me as very
singular, you were so positive in your denial of the fact, and spoke
with such entire confidence that I could not doubt the correctness of what you said, and accordingly, when Mr. Green called
again to see me on the subject, I told him that he had been mis-
informed. He still insisted, however, that the facts were as he
had stated, and that I would ultimately find out he was correct. 328
After a lapse of several weeks, Mr. Green again came to the
department, and not only repeated what he had previously asserted,
but added that a large quantity of shot had actually been sent
down to the arsenal at Fort Monroe, from the Tredegar Works.
I requested him to make the statement in writing, as I was determined that the matter should be fully investigated. He promised
to do so, and a day or two after I received his letter of the 5th
instant. I sent for you, and read this letter to you; after I had
read it through, I asked you "What do you say to this, General?"
Your reply was, "that there was not a word of truth in it; that
it was false from beginning to end," or words to that effect. I 329
again and again questioned you closely on this subject; suggested
how improbable it was that such a story should be fabricated;
that there must be some mistake in the matter. You persisted,
however, in positively affirming that the whole story was false;
that no shot was making or had been made, and no contract entered into for making them. I concluded by directing you to
submit a report to me on the subject.

You said "I have already made my report; I make it now. What further report do you want." I insisted, however, on your submitting a formal report in writing, and you said you would do so.

A day or two after this conversation, you entered my office, 330
accompanied by a gentleman, whom you introduced as Mr. Anderson, of Richmond. As soon as you were seated, you told me
that Mr. Anderson was the owner of the Tredegar Iron Works,
at Richmond, Virginia, and that you had brought him in order
that he might explain to me that matter of the shot. I told you
that I did not wish explanations from Mr. Anderson, but from
you, and I must decline receiving any from him. You answered,
that "as Mr. Anderson was the person with whom the contract
was made, you had supposed he could explain it better than you
could," or words to that effect. This was the first intimation I
had received from you that any such contract had been made. I 331
expressed some surprise at this, and added that I would hear no
explanation on that subject from Mr. Anderson, or from any one
except yourself; that what I had asked for was a report in writing

from *you*, and that I would accept nothing as a substitute for that report. You replied that I should have a report. Mr. Anderson
332 then remarked that it was hard that he should not be permitted to offer explanations in a matter in which he had a personal interest, and went on to say that he made the shot under a contract entered into in good faith on his part; that he had made all his arrangements to fulfill it; had made and actually delivered a portion of the shot, &c. &c. I replied that if he had any claims arising out of any contract made with the department, he could present them and they should be promptly considered; and he might then offer all the explanations he deemed proper; but that no such claim was now before me, the question now was simply
333 whether an order of the department had been obeyed by its officers; whether reports made to it by one of its officers were false or correct; and this was a matter with which he had nothing to do.

You then rose to leave the room; as you did so, I observed, "General, you will immediately issue an order to Colonel Huger to receive no more shot or shells until further orders from the department."

You answered, "that was hardly necessary, you took it for granted that no more would be received." I immediately answered, "No sir; you have already taken too much for granted
334 in this matter; you took it for granted that no contract had been made; you took it for granted that no shot had been made or delivered after you had been positively assured of the contrary. Now henceforward, I wish you to take nothing for granted, but to issue a positive order to Colonel Huger to receive no more shot." You said it should be done, and left the office. Mr. Anderson remained for a few moments longer in the office, and again attempted to offer explanations; but I requested him to submit what he had to say in writing. In the course of his remarks, however, he mentioned that the contract under which he had
335 made the shot, was made by Dr. Carmichael with Colonel Huger. A few days afterwards, your report on Mr. Green's letter was submitted. I was surprised. I was surprised to find, however, that no explanation was offered of the fact, that the report now made by you was entirely inconsistent with your letter of the 27th January last, and with the verbal reports which you had over and over again made to me. I determined to seek elsewhere for this explanation. I accordingly directed Colonel Huger to repair forthwith to the department; he did so, and made a statement, a copy of which is herewith communicated. From this statement,
336 it would seem that you were apprised of the order to Carmichael to make five hundred tons of shot, a few days after it was given, and that you approved of it; and that you were also informed that the order had been assigned or its execution entrusted to Mr. Anderson, of the Tredegar works. It seems too, that the contract with Carmichael was made a few days after I had positively

refused, in your presence, to make one with him, or to recognize
a verbal one which he said had been entered into between him
and a previous head of the department. 337

I would be happy to receive any explanations or any additional
evidence you may wish to offer in relation to this matter.

Very respectfully, your ob't serv't,

C. M. CONRAD,
Secretary of War.

Bt. Brig. Gen'l GEO. TALCOTT.

Statement of Colonel Huger in relation to a quantity of shot
and shells said to have been made by Mr. Joseph R. Anderson,
of Richmond, Virginia, under a contract made by him with Capt. 338
Huger.

Witness says: That on the 8th November last, Dr. Carmichael
of Virginia, came to the arsenal at Fort Monroe, whereof he,
witness, was in command, from Washington, and delivered to
witness a letter, dated the 6th of that month, from General Talcott, authorizing witness to purchase shot and shells; of which
letter a copy is enclosed in witness's letter to the head of the
Ordnance Bureau, dated 17th inst. Whereupon, witness immediately gave to said Carmichael the order, whereof a copy is also
enclosed in said letter. 339

A few days after said order was given, witness came to this
city and informed General Talcott of the order he had given
Carmichael; does not recollect that General Talcott said anything in particular when he communicated the fact to him; while
witness was in this city, he received a letter from Captain Stone
(whom he had left in command of the arsenal), in which Captain S. informed witness that he had just received a letter from
Mr. Anderson, of Richmond, enclosing a power of attorney from
Carmichael to him (Anderson), authorizing him to execute the
order for him, Carmichael; Capt. Stone desired to be instructed
what course to adopt in the matter; witness directed Capt. S. to 340
return the power of attorney to Mr. Anderson, and inform him
that he considered the power of attorney, as in substance, an assignment of the order, and that Mr. Carmichael had no right to
make such a transfer, and that he, witness, would not recognize
it; thinks Mr. Anderson subsequently wrote him one, or perhaps two letters, in which he claimed the right to fill the order;
witness, however, persisted in denying his right to do so, and
advised him to settle the matter with the department before he
made any shot or shells,; this occurred towards the end of November; witness, before leaving the city and returning to the
arsenal, informed General Talcott of the letter he had received 341
from Captain Stone, and of his answer thereto; General Talcott
did not make any particular remark, but seemed to approve of
his (witness) course in the matter; nothing further occurred
until some time in February, when a quantity of 32 pound shot

were sent down to the arsenal by Mr. Anderson; witness did not
receive the shot, but allowed them to be landed, and had them
piled up; he did not in so doing, intend to admit the right of
Anderson to execute the order to Carmichael, but thought it was
a doubtful matter, and that he would leave it to be settled with
the department; he gave no receipt for the shot; did not enter
342 them upon the books of the arsenals; no money was asked for,
and no estimates made by him (witness) with a view to payment of them; the practice at the arsenal had always been to
prepare such estimates, and to pay for munitions of war, as fast
as they were delivered; witness left the arsenal on leave of absence towards the latter part of February, and did not return
there until a few days ago; on his return he found the letter from
the head of the bureau of the 11th inst., directing him to make a
report on this subject, and in preparing to execute this order,
learned for the first time, that during his absence more shot had
been sent down to the arsenal by Mr. Anderson; they had been
landed and stored away, but no receipt had been given for them;
343 they had not been entered on the books; no estimates prepared,
no money demanded or paid; witness omitted to state, that some
time before Mr. Anderson sent down to him the power of attorney above referred to, he received a letter from Mr. Kemble, of
the West Point foundry, wishing to know whether the order given
by witness to Carmichael could be transferred, and witness replied
that it could not be transferred; witness says he had previously
on other occasions received authority from the head of the bureau
to order small quantities of munitions of war, but had never been
344 authorized to purchase a large quantity until the letter of the 6th
Nov. was sent to him; being asked what he understood to be
meant by the order to purchase the shot and shells only "in open
market," says that he understood by that simply that he should
purchase them on as reasonable terms as he could procure them;
he never communicated to General Talcott *officially* the order he
had given to Carmichael; he informed him of it, however, privately, as above stated; does not recollect whether Gen. Talcott
was informed that shot had been sent to the arsenal by Anderson
under the order given to Carmichael; says he was pretty certain
345 he was not informed of it; does not know whether a copy of the
order of this department of the 29th January last, prohibiting the
different heads of bureaus from making contracts for sums exceeding $2,000, was ever sent to the arsenal; has no recollection
of ever having seen it; it may, however, have been sent down
during his absence; a few days ago, witness received a letter
from Mr. Anderson, requesting him to make estimates for the
shot he had delivered; this letter was dated at Washington; it
did not mention that he, Anderson, had had an interview with
the Secretary of War, and that an order had been issued by the
346 department to witness to receive no shot under the contract with
Carmichael; witness did not answer the letter immediately, and

a few days afterwards an order from the department was received, directing him, witness, not to receive any shot or shells
from any foundry or manufacture; witness then sent Mr. Ander- 347
son a copy of this order as an answer to his letter; if witness
had not received the order, he would not have estimated for the
payment of the shot, but would have referred him to the department.

2nd Examination.

April 25th, 1851.

Witness produced a letter from Capt. Stone to himself referred
to in his deposition, marked A, and extract from answer made
by Stone to Anderson's letter to him marked B, also letter from
Anderson to witness, dated Richmond, December 10th, 1850, a
copy of which is retained, marked C, also a letter from Gouve- 348
neur Kemble to witness, marked D, answer of witness, marked
E, and reply of Kemble, marked F.

Witness made the contract with Carmichael on the day he
came to the arsenal. The details were arranged between Carmichael and Capt. Stone. Witness being indisposed. Did not
make proposals to receive them from any one else. Considered
the price agreed to he paid for them, low. Being asked if he
knew of any reason why Carmichael should go right from the
department with a letter from the chief of the bureau authorizing
him to make the contract instead of making it here with the
head of the bureau himself, says he knows of no reason, never 349
thought any thing about it.

It was distinctly understood, when the order was given to
Carmichael that the shot and shells should be made at the foundry at Fredericksburg, owned by Carmichael and a man by the
name of Wellford. Witness had tried the shot and shells made at
that foundry and they proved of excellent quality. This was his
reason for desiring them to be made there, and Carmichael stated
as his reason for being anxious to get the order that he desired to
put the foundry, (which had been suspended for some time past,)
once more in operation.

He consideres that Carmichael practiced a gross deception in 350
attempting to transfer the order to any other foundry.

BENJ. HUGER,
Bt. Col.

(A.)

Fort Monroe, Nov. 22nd, 1850.

My dear Col,—I enclose you a treasury draft with the necessary papers to sign.

This morning brought me a letter from Mr. Anderson enclosing
a power of *Attorney from Dr. Carmichael* for making the shot 351
ordered at Wellford foundry! Is not that a beautiful opera-
on for the Doctor? He said most expressly that he wanted the
contract for the sole purpose of starting the foundry: and now

he has turned the whole order over to the Tredegar Works. Shall I put the power of Attorney on file and send up the guages
352 as Anderson requested? I have been firing this morning, and the results, &c. xx experiments with spherical case shot.

Yours,

(Signed,) C. P. STONE,
Bt. Captain.

(B.)

FORT MONROE ARSENAL,
November 26th, 1850.

J. R. ANDERSON, ESQ., *Richmond.*

353 I am instructed by Col. Huger now in Washington, to return you the power of Attorney issued to you by Dr. E. Carmichael and to say that he (Col. H.) thinks Dr. C. had, under the circumstances, no right to transfer his order for shot without first consulting him and obtaining his consent. * * *

Yours &c.

(Signed.) C. P. STONE,
Bt. Capt. Ordnance.

(C.)

(*Private.*)

RICHMOND, Dec. 10, 1850.

354 My dear Col.—Your letter of the 6th inst. was duly received and I am very much astonished to learn that Dr. C. has stated what he did to you and the General about the place at which the shot were to be made.

I beg that you will allow me to make you acquainted with some circumstances, a simple narrative of which, without any comment, will I trust, fully justify my course in obtaining the control of the order and without waiting to communicate with you which I desired to do.

I was aware that Dr. C. had a claim on the government for a large contract for shot and shells, for he had brought the papers
355 to me several months ago and solicited me to unite with him in promoting and prosecuting this claim, proposing that I should be equally interested in it. I unconditionally declined the proposition, being unwilling to connect myself or establishment with a claim for a contract which I believed to have been improperly promised. Still it appeard to me, the faith of the government had been pledged, and I thought it quite likely that a succeeding administration, seeing the importance of preserving the credit of the government intact, would direct the contract to be given to
356 him. His rights too, were sustained by high legal authority. Upon my declining his proposition, Dr. C. asked me if I would be willing if he succeeded, to have the work done for him at the "Tredegar Works" I replied unhesitatingly that I would. He

said that it would aid him very much, and asked me to put it in
writing, which I did and gave him the paper.

When in Washington a few weeks ago, I met a friend who told 357
me that Dr. Carmichael had succeeded in getting his contract,
and that he mentioned it to me because he was aware that I was
to have the work done.

I returned home, and a day or two afterwards Dr. C. called at my office, handed me your order, and said he had but a few minutes to remain; that he had several offers for it, one of which he showed me, and that unless I agreed upon terms at once he would go north the next day to sell his contract.

I had reason to believe that he had represented to the department that I was to make the shot, and if not, I believed that you
would be glad to have the order in the hands of a friend, instead 358
of being hawked about to every blast furnace in the country; and
above all, I felt naturally very desirous to have the work for my
establishment, and I granted him such terms as were satisfactory
to him, and made him an advance much heavier than I would
under other circumstances have made, as I had known him long
and his family well, and knew how greatly in want of funds he
was; necessary to enable him to get to New Orleans.

Now knowing me well enough, I hope to feel that you lose
nothing at least, by the order being executed by myself instead of
Dr. C. I hope you will not hesitate to grant me every facility; 359
and I am certainly desirous of consulting your own convenience
as to funds; I would like to deliver some 10 or 15,000 shot as
soon as made, and I will afterwards confer with you as to the
delivery of the others.

Please write me saying if I shall, and send me a pair of 32 pdr. guages.

Yours truly,

(Signed,) J. R. ANDERSON.

As to the words of the power of attorney, I endeavored to
make it agree with the order. I have the order among my papers, 360
however, and no doubt you have a copy of it, which will be all
that is necessary for your guidance, as the power of attorney
makes *no* transfer, but is merely a matter between the principal
and agent, designed to show you that the power to sign his name
is delegated to me as agent; it appears to me that the terms of
it are not essential, except so far as they designate the order under
which I am acting. I put the papers in this form, believing it
would be more agreeable to you than a proposition to transfer
the order or contract on your books. Officially or otherwise, you
are not aware of any transfer or sale of the contract, and there- 361
fore, you may, to me as you did to Mr. Kemble, decline to assent
to a transfer. But I do not ask for a transfer. I deliver the shot
in the *name of Dr. Carmichael*, and settle for him in *his name*.
Just in this way I filled an order Mr. Tucker had from the Bureau

of Ordnance, &c. I hope this will satisfy you. Please drop me a
362 line by return mail as to delivery of 10 or 15,000 shot and guages

Yours, J. R. ANDERSON.

Endorsement.—Ans'd Dec. 18. No doubt the matter can be managed if he will write to Gen'l T. or Maynadier; notify him I will want shells or S. C.; will write him hereafter.

(D.)

(*Private.*)

363 COLD SPRING, 17*th Nov.*, 1850.

Dear Gen'l,—Dr. Carmichael, of Richmond, has written to me enclosing a copy of a letter from Col. Huger ordering 500 tons of 32 pdr. shot, deliverable at Old Point Comfort; offering the order to me for our execution and delivery according to the terms therein specified. Of course the Doctor is to take the lion's share of profits, but it would enable me to keep our moulders together during the winter, when the work of the department generally falls off; and therefore, if an arrangement by which the order should be transferred to me would meet the approbation of the department, I should try to make one with him.

364 I shall write to him to this effect, more particularly because there appears to be some irregularity in the transaction that I do not understand; and I would ask the favor of you to inform me as early as possible, whether there would be any objection on your part, and if not, how I had best manage with him, whether through a special power of attorney from him, or by transfer of the order in any other manner.

Very sincerely, yours,

GOUV. KEMBLE.

GEN'L TALCOTT, *Ordnance Department*, *Washington.*

365 Please direct to the care of
William Kemble, New York.

(E.)

WASHINGTON, *November* 21*st*, 1850.

My dear sir,—General Talcott has referred your letter of the 17th instant to me.

Neither General T. or myself consider the order to Doctor Carmichael for a supply of shot, assignable in the manner he proposes. Dr. Carmichael was interested in a foundry near Fredericksburg, Virginia, and supplies of shot and shells for Fort
366 Monroe having heretofore been procured there. In giving him the order, a copy of which he sent you, it was understood that the work was to be done at that foundry, which could only turn them out in limited quantities as required, and as I had means to pay for them.

I was only authorized by General T. to estimate for funds to pay for them, from time to time, as I required them, and my stating the whole amount that would be required was for the 367
purpose of letting the founder (Mr. Wellford, who Dr. C. told me would have charge of the works), make his arrangements for materials, &c., not that I expected him to deliver the whole amount immediately.

Under these circumstances I am not authorized to consent to the transfer of the order to Dr. C. in the manner he proposes.

I am, truly yours,

(Signed,) BENJ. HUGER.

Gouv. Kemble, Esq.

(F.) 368

Cold Spring, 23*d* *Nov.*, 1850.

Dear Col.—I have your letter of the 21st; there seemed to be something out of the way, that did not appear upon the face of this business with Carmichael, which caused me to enquire further before answering him directly; but your letter contains no stipulation in relation to the delivery, further than its taking place at Old Point, and I think, therefore, that it may cause you some trouble; for he is not bound to have the shot made at Fredericksburg or any where else in particular; besides, if I am not mistaken, 369
Mr. Wellford is dead, and Dr. Carmichael has long since disposed of his interest in the foundry; let me know, therefore, the times of payment, and the amounts that would be convenient to you, and if I can arrange the affair with him I will, for it is better that this letter of yours, which is a positive order, should be in the hand of a friend.

Yours, faithfully,

GOUVENIR KEMBLE.

Col. Huger, U. S. A., *Washington.*

370

Fort Monroe, Virginia,
November 23*d*, 1850.

My dear Col.—Yours of the 21st is received. My impressions received from Dr. Carmichael's conversation certainly were that the shot were to be cast at Wellford's foundry, and that the very object of getting the order was the starting of the foundry with certain work for the first year. Indeed, he expressly stipulated that an allowance should be made in the price, for the transportation from Fredericksburg here, and an allowance was made for that transportation, of $1·50 per ton—that is to say, the shot were rated at enough per lb. above the contract price, to cover the transportation at that rate. I recollect asking him too, if his 371
foundry was not the old Wellford's, and getting a reply in the affirmative.

His turning over the order to Mr. Anderson without consulting

you, is exceedingly unfair; for I pointed out to him the shot and shells lately received from Richmond, and criticised them. If he
372 had any idea of turning the order over to A., he ought in common honesty to have said so, and asked your consent.

I mentioned yesterday that I doubted the correctness of our conclusions against the capabilities of the 8-inch spherical cases, and this morning I have proved them wrong, as you will see from the enclosed table of this morning's firing. Four of the S. C. shot fired with the discharge of 3 lbs., were condemned on account of suspected weakness, and one of those fired with $3\frac{1}{4}$ lbs. had been fired before. I shall test them more severely on Monday or Tuesday.

373 I am very glad the tige muskets are to be taken up. The pointed form of the tige is something new, since my visit to France. Do let them have a fair chance before the board, and do tell me where the one you have came from. Has General T. allowed some cit to bring up the thing before he took hold of it?

Laidley is here, but I have not yet seen him, (10 o'clock.) I shall go soon.

Mr. Anderson asked in his letter to have guages sent up immediately; I wrote him in reply that as I was very confident you had not intended the order to be transferred from Wellford's foun-
374 dry, I must first receive your instructions.

What an outrage was that relieving Capt. B. from Fayetteville! Had he mixed actively in politics? And now that Dyer has been sent there, how much better off is Kingsbury by the change?

ORDNANCE DEPARTMENT,
Washington, May 3d, 1851.

HON. C. M. CONRAD, *Secretary of War:*

Sir,—I have the honor to acknowledge the receipt of your letter of the 1st inst., with the accompanying papers; all of which I have attentively read and duly considered. A recapitulation of
375 the facts connected with the subject of your letter, putting them with their dates in regular order, will be, I conceive, the most proper mode of replying. Their full exhibit will furnish an explanation satisfactory to me, and I trust to the Secretary of War also.

Dr. Carmichael, in the spring of 1850, claimed a promise of Ex-President Tyler, for a certain amount of castings to be given him to make by contract. His claim was not deemed valid by me. Secretary Crawford also rejected it, and in November last he was disposed to bring it again before the Secretary of War.

I accompanied him at his urgent request, and was present an
376 fully recognized the justice of the Secretary in its third rejection. It was not because I considered his claim valid, but because he really had no claim, that I gave him the paper addressed to Col. Huger, authorizing the latter to purchase, in open market, shot and shells to a reasonable extent, from time to time, thereby

giving Dr. Carmichael a chance to make a bargain, if he could, to furnish *some shot and shells*, which I had at that time an undoubted right to do, and if I was put on oath I should say that I supposed he would succeed in getting a small order. The paper to Col. Huger reads as follows:

"ORDNANCE DEPARTMENT,
Washington, 6*th November*, 1850. 378

"COL. B. HUGER, *Fort Monroe Arsenal:*

"Sir,—It may be well to provide more shot and shells, from time to time, for the post of Fort Monroe, and for this purpose you are authorized to procure them to a reasonable extent, if, as I suppose, (the price of iron being now so low) they can be had on favorable terms. You will make the necessary estimates of funds to meet the deliveries as they occur; they should be procured by open purchase only.

"I am, Sir, respectfully, &c. 379
"G. TALCOTT,
"*Bt. Br. Genl., Col. Ordnance.*"

I heard nothing of the Doctor's success in the matter, until I received a letter from Mr. Kemble, dated 17th Nov., 1850, which is found appended to the statement of Col. Huger, marked D, addressed to *me*, and not to Col. Huger, as stated by the Secretary of War. Col. Huger had but just arrived here, and was acting as a member of the Board for the trial of small arms. The letter was either handed to Col. Huger or sent to him by me, and I
desired him to reply to it, as I knew nothing of the matter. He 380
told me what he had done, and if I made no comment it was because I was astonished at the recital. He, however, replied to that letter as desired, and repudiated the conduct of Dr. Carmichael, and here I supposed the great contract which had been noised about, was ended. I have not the dates of my conversations with the Secretary of War, in relation to the wants of the department for shot and shells, but let the several times be when they may, the answers were correct and true in relation to contracts or large supplies. He never told me that he wished to
give any man a contract, and when I heard that Carmichael had 381
one for furnishing 500 tons, I scouted the idea, taking for granted that no officer of my corps could so misconstrue authority to make "open purchases" of shot, or could convert my letter of the 6th November into authority to give such an order.

It may not be out of place here to state that a copy of the War Department order of the 29th January, 1851, was not sent to Col. Huger, because it is only directed to and contains instructions for the government of the heads of the Quarter Master General's, the Subsistence and the Ordnance Department. It may
have been an error in me to take Mr. Anderson to the Secretary 382
of War on the subject of his own doings, but I had just received the letter of T. Green, with directions to report, which I could

not do until I heard from Col. Huger, who had gone to South Carolina on leave, and his return had not been reported. An-
383 derson happened here by accident, and told me all that had been done, and from him I first heard that shot had been delivered. I simply supposed the Secretary of War would be willing to hear the facts of the case from him, so far as he was concerned, and that much time might be saved; but I found that he was indisposed to talk with him on the subject. In some stage of this matter, I may have displayed too much tenderness for a brother officer; in such a case I would sooner *suffer wrong* than *do wrong*. I now insist that I did not authorize the order as given to Dr. Carmichael, and that Col. Huger in construing my letter into
384 authority for him to give such an order, committed an error of judgment; the order to Carmichael was never approved by me. When Col. Huger informed me of Anderson's claim under his assignment, and of his action in the case, not acknowledging, but virtually repudiating it, I approved that, and heard no more about it until my report to you of the 27th January, 1851; that report stated that no contracts had been made for shot from the last appropriations; that no shot had been furnished; that there were no contracts for shot made by this department unfulfilled, and that none were contemplated. With the information I had
385 when that report was made, all this was strictly true. I had then and have since recognized no contract, nor do I now. I knew not that Mr. Anderson had gone on to fill Col. Huger's order. This information was received by me subsequently, and was stated in my report of the 19th April. Both reports stated the facts as known to me when they were made, and all the facts, as is my invariable custom in reporting on calls for information from the War Department. I saw then no inconsistency between the reports, or between them and my verbal communications, requiring explanation, and I am compelled to say that I see none
386 now. The foregoing will show, I think, that although I had no objection to Dr. Carmichael's obtaining work on shot and shells from time to time, to a reasonable extent, if he could make a bargain with Col. Huger on satisfactory terms, I never gave him an order, or authorized or approved the one he received, and that in all my subsequent conversations and reports to you on the subject I had reason to suppose that Col. Huger had repudiated Dr. Carmichael's transfer of his order; that no evidence of any deliveries or estimates of funds in payment of work under that order had been received, and that consequently I had good reason
387 to believe that the whole matter had ended with Col. Huger's repudiation of the transfer, and Dr. Carmichael's inability otherwise to execute the order.

I am, sir, repectfully, your ob't serv't,

G. TALCOTT,

Bt. Brig'r Gen'l, Col. of Ordnance.

After the reading of the foregoing papers, the witness said: In my communication with Gen. Talcott in the presence of Mr. Anderson, before stated, I said, the question is whether an order of the department has been disobeyed, or whether false reports 388
have been made to the department; I will explain what I meant by this disobedience to which I then referred; shortly after (immediately after, I believe) receiving the written report of the 27th January, understanding that contracts had been made by the Ordnance Department without the sanction of the Secretary (of which fact, however, I know nothing), and not knowing that there was a regulation of that bureau requiring the sanction of the Secretary to all contracts, I determined to make such a regulation, and accordingly prepared one; it struck me, however, that if it was addressed to the Ordnance Department alone, it might be offensive to General Talcott, and I made it applicable 389
to all the bureaux which make contracts for supplies, although it is not so necessary for the others, as few of their contracts, I believe, are made in this city; I accordingly issued an order on the 29th January, requiring that all contracts made by any of the bureaux in this city, exceeding $2,000, should be first submitted to the Secretary; when I had the conversation with Gen. Talcott, and learnt that shot was making, and being at that time ignorant at what time the contract had been made, I supposed it possible it had been made since the adoption of that regulation, and *that* was the disobedience I referred to; as the contract was made, or what was done was done prior to the 29th January, it was not a 390
disobedience of that order.

And then at 3 o'clock the court adjourned, (and on account of the amount of the record of this day's proceedings.) to meet to-morrow at 12 o'clock.

---

12 o'clock, July 2, 1851.

The court met pursuant to adjournment.

Present all the members, the Judge Advocate and General Talcott.

The proceedings of yesterday were read over. 391

Charles M. Conrad, Secretary of War, a witness for the prosecution.

Direct examination continued:

The witness said before proceeding further with his testimony this day, he desired to correct an error in his testimony yesterday. There had been two copies sent to him by General Talcott of the letter of General Talcott to Col. Huger, dated 6th Nov. To one of these copies was a note appended in the hand-writing 392
of General Talcott. Witness supposed yesterday that this copy with the note appended to it, was the copy sent to him in the report of General Talcott, dated the 27th January. He was now

quite satisfied that this copy was sent in the report from the
Ordnance Bureau, dated the 19th April, on Mr. Green's letter;
394 and the other copy, with no such note, was the copy accompanying the report of the 27th January. The witness desired to
make this correction, and if necessary to show the evidence on
which it was made. But the defence had no doubt of its accuracy,
and admitted the correction now made.

Q. Did you at any time, before the 1st Nov. 1850, give to
General Talcott any instructions or authority to make contracts
or purchases for the Ordnance Department, without obtaining
your previous sanction thereto. If so, state when, and, how?
A. No sir, I gave no such authority or instructions.

Q. Did you give General Talcott any instructions in regard to
395 a contract or contracts, about this time, the 1st November, 1850,
I mean other than the testimony you have already given, in regard to the Carmichael contract? *A.* I find, that a few days
prior to the conversation between Dr. Carmichael and myself,
referred to in my previous testimony, that is to say on the 24th
October, 1850, a letter was addressed to me by Johnstone and
Ashton of Conn., requesting to be allowed to renew a contract
previously made with the department, for making pistols. This
letter was referred to the Ordnance Bureau, on the 24th October,
General Talcott reported on this letter, that the writer of the
letter had contracted to furnish 30,000 pistols, and that the con-
396 tract would expire in about a year, and that they desired an extension of the contract. He said, "this course has frequently
been pursued in like cases. The only question, however, is
whether new proposals shall be invited, or the old contract be
extended, and this is a point for your decision." This I quote
from the letter which I hold in my hand. I find on this report
the following endorsement in my hand-writing, dated the 5th Nov.
It is not deemed expedient at present at all events to renew the
contract with Messrs. Johnson and Ashton, trials and experiments are now being made of various species of pistol, some of
recent invention; and besides, it is deemed safer considering the
397 length of time which has elapsed since the contract with the above
named individuals was made, to advertise for proposals for a new
contract.

(Signed.) C. M. CONRAD,
Secretary of War.

This order by an endorsement on it, appears to have been received at the Ordnance Department on the same day. Perhaps
it is proper that I should add, that some months after, General
Talcott brought one of the individuals, with whom the contract
had been made to the office, and stated that they were young me-
398 chanics, who had embarked on this undertaking without means,
that they had just put up extensive and costly works, relying
upon the contracts being extended, as it was customary to ex-

tend them, and that the work they had done was of excellent quality and as cheap, or cheaper than it could be done elsewhere. I think also, the trials and experiments, I had mentioned in fire 399
arms, had taken place in the meanwhile; and in consideration of these circumstances, and the verbal recommendation of General Talcott in that conversation, I authorized him to extend the contract for a limited amount. The paper here presented, shows the last application of the parties, the recommendation of the Colonel of Ordnance, and the decision of the Secretary of War above referred to.

MIDDLETOWN, CON., *March 21st*, 1851.

GENL. G. TALCOTT:

Sir,—The undersigned, partners in the firm of Henry Ashton 400
& Co., do hereby agree that an extension of the pistol contract, as applied for, shall be given to Ira N. Johnson, they having made an arrangement to the satisfaction of all the parties interested in the establishment.

Respectfully your ob't serv'ts,
HENRY ASHTON
SILVESTER C. BAILY,
IRA N. JOHNSON,
PETER H. ASHTON,
JOHN NORTH. 401

Endorsements on this letter as follows:

HENRY ASHTON and others.

MIDDLETOWN, CONN., *March 21st*, 1851.

Agree that an extension of the pistol contract be granted to Ira N. Johnson.

"Respectfully submitted to the Secretary of War for his information in regard to the agreement among the parties interested, in case he should determine to extend the contract."

G. TALCOTT, 402
Bt. Brig. Genl., Col. of Ordnance.

ORDNANCE DEPARTMENT, *March, 25th*, 1851.

Received, March 24th, 1851:

If all the parties interested in the manufactory have signed the within consent, the chief of the Ordnance Bureau will take measures to renew the contract for a limited supply of pistols.

26th March, 1851.

C. M. CONRAD,
Sec'y of War, War Department. 403

Received March 28th, 1851.

See letter to Ira N. Johnson this date.

Q. When General Talcott, as you state, a few days after his report to you of the 27th January, 1851, explained to you verbally the object and meaning of his letter to Col. Huger, dated 6th November, 1850, of which he had sent you a copy in his said

report, did he tell you how Col. Huger had construed that letter,
or what he had done under it? *A.* No sir; he never made the
slightest allusion then, or at any time, to any action having been
404 taken under his letter to Col. Huger, except, as I stated in my
examination yesterday, he did at one time say to me, that perhaps
Col. Huger might procure some inconsiderable quantity of shot or
shells for experiments.

Q. Did he never inform you of the existence of that order to
Carmichael before the visit of Mr. Anderson? *A.* He never informed me of it at all, that I recollect, until his report of the 19th
April; the first I ever heard of an order or contract, (for I did
not know at that time it was in the form of an order,) was from
Mr. Green, a day or two before his letter to me of the 5th April;
405 and it was repeated in his letter of the 5th April. In the interview with Mr. Anderson, I said to General Talcott, then there is
a contract, or there is shot making, to which he answered, "It
seems so." Mr. Anderson mentioned the fact, that it was an
order from Huger to Carmichael.

Q. When did you first learn of this letter from Col. Huger to
General Talcott, reporting the number of 32 pdr. balls which
might be provided for the armament of Fort Monroe? *A.* On
Saturday evening last, I was informed by a gentleman who is not
in any way connected with the department, that he had strong rea-
406 sons for believing that a letter existed on the records of the department from Col. Huger to General Talcott, in relation to the subject
of these shot. I informed the Judge Advocate of that fact, and requested him to apply to the acting head of the Bureau of Ordnance,
whether any such letter was there. On Monday morning last,
when I arrived at the department, the acting head of the bureau,
handed me the letter; that was the first I ever saw of it.

Q. Upon what points in Mr. Green's letter was General Talcott directed to report to you? *A.* The only point upon which I
wished any report, and the only subject upon which General
407 Talcott and myself coversed, was in relation to that part of it
which stated that shot were being made at the Tredegar Works,
in Richmond, and that some had been delivered at the Monroe
arsenal.

Q, In your letter to General Talcott, you state that you enquired of him about the actual making of shot and shell at the
Tredegar Works some time after his report of you of the 27th
January, and in your testimony yesterday you appear to refer
this conversation to some point of time previous to that report
of the 27th January; how does your recollection now stand on
408 this point, or is it positive? *A.* My recollection of these various
conversations with General Talcott is quite distinct, but I have had
some difficulty in fixing the precise dates at which they severally
occurred, having made no memoranda at the time, and not supposing at the time that I should ever be called upon to testify
in regard to them; the first conversation, in which I told him

that I was informed that a contract existed and was held by some one at Richmond, took place, I am pretty confident, some time
in December; the next action of the department, of the date of 409
which there can be no doubt, is the order of the 20th January; in regard to the conversation in which I informed him that shot had been made, and was piled up at the foundry, my memory is not accurate, and I can find no memoranda to aid it; when I wrote the letter of the 1st May, to General Talcott, I supposed that that conversation occurred subsequently to the 27th January, and that may possibly be correct; subsequent reflection, however, led me to believe that this conversation occurred a short time prior to the letter of the 20th January, and may
possibly in part have occasioned that letter. 410

Cross examination:

Q. Be pleased to fix as nearly as you can, the date of your first enquiry of General Talcott as to whether supplies of shot and shell were required by the department? *A.* I have endeavored to fix my memory on that point, but can not do so with any degree of accuracy; shortly after I took charge of the department, which was on the 16th or 17th of August, and during the five or six following months, applications were made by various persons to make shot; some Members of Congress, I think, but I am not
certain (I know they did afterwards), spoke on behalf of their 411
constituents; one of the first, if not the first application, was made by Mr Green, but I can not state the time at which his first application was made to me; my first enquiry of General Talcott was probably made shortly after the first application was made to me; probably the same or the next day.

Q. Is it your impression that this enquiry was made in the month of August or September, or what month? *A.* It was certainly not made in August; it may have been made in September, or early in October; I was absent from the city during a
great part of October; my impression is rather that it was made 412
in November, after my return from the north, and if made in November, it was probably made subsequent to the 6th Nov.; I can not say that there are any acts on which this impression is founded; my first impression was that it was prior to that date, but now I think it may have been after.

Q. Are you clear that you repeated that enquiry more than once, and if you did, at what intervals, as nearly as you can fix them? *A.* I am very confident that I repeated it, though at what intervals I can not say; I recollect stating to General Talcott that I
was very frequently asked that question, and that he replied that 413
there was an ample supply on hand; at what precise time this conversation occurred I can not say; it was probably some time in the winter.

And here, at 3 o'clock, the court adjourned, to meet to-morrow morning at 10 o'clock.

Thursday, 3d July, 10 o'clock, 1851.

The court met pursuant to adjournment. Present, all the
414 members, the Judge Advocate and General Talcott.

The proceedings of yesterday were read over.

C. M. Conrad, Secretary of War, a witness on the part of the prosecution.

Cross examination continued.

Q. Were your inquiries of General Talcott as to the wants of
the service, directed to ascertain whether small quantities of shot
would probably be required, from time to time during the year,
at one or more of the arsenals, or were they not suggested by
applications to furnish large or contract supplies and confined to
415 that subject only? *A.* My applications to General Talcott were
general; no reference was made to quantity, nor to the mode of
procuring them.

Q. Was not Mr. Green's application to you, in behalf of Mr.
F. B. Deane for a contract to furnish large supplies of shot and
shell? and did not this occasion your call upon General Talcott?
A. Mr. Green did not refer to any quantity. I presume he would
have preferred a large contract to a small one; but he never intimated that he would not take a small one. His application did
occasion one of the calls that I made on General Talcott, but his
416 was not the only application which caused me to converse with
General Talcott on that subject.

Q. Referring now to your testimony in chief, that upon Mr.
Green's first application you enquired of Gen. Talcott, "whether
the department would be in want of shot *during the current fiscal year*, which *terminated yesterday*," (30th June,) and that you
were answered that the supply for the year was ample, are you
not now satisfied, on reflection, that you could not have repeated
the *same question* on several occasions within a short period, and
may not that impression have grown out of your conversations
417 with the applicants? *A.* I do not say that I repeated the same
question in a direct form for information, considering his first
answer, which I well remembered, as satisfactory; but a number of
applications, some verbal and some in writing, being made to me
from time to time for shot and shells, I mentioned these applications to him, sometimes rather, perhaps, as a source of annoyance,
for I had many of them, and some very importunate, with a view,
probably, to ascertain whether he was positive that the department would not be making shot, in order that I might give the
applicants a satisfactory answer.

Q. Were not your enquiries of General Talcott, touching the
418 making and delivery of shot by Mr. Anderson, directed solely to
ascertain whether such making and delivery were under contract
with or by authority of the Ordnance Bureau? *A.* My inquiry
was general, whether any shot was making at Mr. Anderson's
works for the department, taking it for granted, of course, that
none could be making without his knowledge and authority.

Q. Did you understand General Talcott's declaration that there
was not a word of truth in Mr. Green's letter, as importing lit- 419
erally that there was no truth in any part of the letter, or
as applying to the assertion or implication that a large quantity
of shot had been made by his order, or with his knowledge or
authority?

The Judge Advocate doubted the strict competency of the testimony which the witness was now applied to, to give. The
question put to General Talcott, the answer of General Talcott, and all the facts which could explain his answer, were before the court. Of the meaning, intent and effect of his answer
the Judge Advocate supposed the court would judge; but he had
no desire to oppose any objection to testimony, and especially to 420
any cross-examination of the present witness.

A. I understood that expression of General Talcott to apply
exclusively to that portion of the letter which speaks of the
making of shot at the Tredegar works for the War Department,
and of the delivery of a portion of them at the Monroe arsenal,
in a word, to all in the letter that relates to the making of shot
for the department, and the authority by which it was done.
Our conversation had no reference to any other part of the letter,
as I had not, after his reports to me, the remotest idea of giving
a contract to Mr. Deane, or to any one else, for making *shot*. I
understood, of course, General Talcott's declaration that there 421
was not a word of truth in the letter which related to the making
of shot at the Tredegar works, to apply to all that was said in
the letter on that subject. He said nothing to qualify his remark
in any manner.

Q. When, some time after General Talcott's report of the 27th
January, enclosing a copy of his letter of 6th November to Col.
Huger, it occurred to you that the large quantity of shot of which
Mr. Green had informed you might have been made under that
order, and you spoke to General Talcott on that subject, was not
your inquiry confined to that point, and was not General Talcott's
reply to this effect, that it was impossible that Colonel Huger 422
could be procuring from the Ordnance Department, under that
order, anything more than such few shot and shells as he might
be wanting for experiments and practice? *A*. My attention was
called to the generality and vagueness of the order, and I called
General Talcott's attention to that point, and asked him to explain what he intended by it, and suggested that possibly Colonel
Huger might construe it to confer authority to make shot. General Talcott seemed to think otherwise, and stated that its object
was to enable Colonel Huger to obtain small quantities, as they
might be required from time to time, for experiments and artillery practice; that it was possible Colonel Huger might be order- 423
ing some such small quantities of trifling value. This is as well
as I recollect the substance of what passed between us; I don't
pretend to repeat the language.

Q. Was the contract of Johnston and Ashton mentioned in your testimony on yesterday a formal written contract, and for what amount? *A.* I know nothing of the original contract (having never seen it) except what is stated in General Talcott's report. I took it for granted that what was there stated was
424 correct.

Q. The language of your authority for extending that contract is, "The chief of the Ordnance Bureau will take measures to renew the contract for a limited supply of pistols." Was there any specification of the amount by you, or did you leave it to his discretion to require the pistols to a reasonable extent; and do you know whether the contract has been renewed, and for what amount? *A.* There was no amount specified by my order as will be seen from it. The words limited supply, which I used, would indicate a less quantity than the original contract. I left the
425 extent of that supply, with that limitation, to General Talcott's discretion. I do not know whether the contract has been extended or not. I have no recollection of any contract having been presented to me for my signature or approbation. I only recollect that some difficulty arose as to the parties with whom the contract should be renewed, the partners in the concern having quarrelled among themselves, in consequence of which the order of the 26th March was given. I do not recollect whether any or what action has been taken by me since that order was given. It is possible a contract may have been presented to me and I
426 may have forgotten it.

Re-examination, by Judge Advocate.

Q. Did you read the whole letter of Mr. Green to General Talcott, and especially did you read these words therein: "Whatever authority for doing this work exists, was probably given by the department, or its officers, to Doctor Ed. H. Carmichael, recently a resident of Richmond, but now of the city of New Orleans. During a recent visit to Richmond I was informed the work was done by Mr. Anderson under an assignment from Dr. Carmichael;" and do you mean to be understood by the defence,
427 in your answer on their cross examination, that you so shaped your inquiries to General Talcott that his answer did not cover and apply directly to that part of the letter? *A.* I will state, sir, that I read the entire letter to General Talcott, as I have stated before, from beginning to end. I certainly did not, in my answer to the question by the defence, mean to be understood as having so shaped my inquiry as not to apply his answer to that portion of Mr. Green's letter contained in this question. I stated that I understood his denial of the truth of what was stated in that letter to apply to all that related to the making of shot at
428 the Tredegar works, and I consider that the order given to Carmichael, and the assignment of that order by Carmichael to Anderson, both of which facts are mentioned in the letter as intimately, connected with the making of shot at the Tredegar works,

which are owned by Mr. Anderson. My attention was particularly drawn to that part of the letter in consequence of what had
previously occurred. I must have laid particular emphasis on 429
that part of the letter, and I recollect that I did.

Q. Do you recollect whether or no you sometimes sent to the
Ordnance Bureau, applications which were made to you for contracts for shot, for reports to you, or for answers to the wri-
ters? *A.* My uniform practice is to refer all letters on the business of the department to the bureau to which the business ap-
pertains, and when applications are verbal, to converse with the
head of the bureau on the subject; of course all applications
in writing made to me on this subject, were sent to the Ordnance
Bureau. 430

Cross examination by defence:

Q. Had your enquiries to which General Talcott replied "I
say there is not a word of truth in it," any other shape than you
have already stated, viz: that after reading the letter you said,
"What do you say to that, General?" *A.* I meant to say that that
was the mode in which I introduced the conversation with General Talcott, after reading to him Mr. Green's letter; but I did
not mean to be understood to say that that was the only question
that I put to him in the conversation on that occasion; on the
contrary, the conversation was a long one, and I put the question 431
in various shapes, having become satisfied that there was some
mystery in this business that required explanation.

John Potts, a witness for the prosecution, being sworn in due
form of law, testified as follows:

Direct examination by Judge Advocate:

Q. What office do you hold in the War Department? *A.*
Chief clerk.

Q. Were you sent by the Secretary of War to General Talcott
to make enquiries of him in regard to shot; if so, say what
enquiry, and what answer he made? *A.* Some short time after I 432
was appointed chief clerk, which was on the 5th March, of this
year, I was sent by the Secretary of War to make some enquiries
in regard to appropriations for shot and shells; I went to the
Ordnance Office and asked the question what balances of appropriations were available for that object; I received the information from the office; General Talcott asked me if we were going
to purchase more shot and shells; I told him I did not know; that
I had left Mr. Green in conversation with the Secretary of War,
and I presumed the enquiry that I was making had connection
with the object of his visit; I asked General Talcott if they 433
wanted shot and shells; his reply was, that they did not; that
there were enough on hand to last till the day of judgment, or
words to that effect.

Q. You say this was some short time after the 5th March, this
year; was it before the 10th April? *A.* I have no means of de-

terming that; I think it was; I think it was shortly after I came into the chief clerkship of the War Department.

Captain William Maynadier, a witness for the prosecution, re-
434 called.

Direct examination renewed:

Q. Did General Talcott, so far as the records of your office show, or you otherwise know, in answer to any of the enquiries to him from the War Department, make any enquiry of Col. Huger or Mr. Anderson, between the 1st January and the 10th April, 1851, in regard to the execution of the order of Huger to Carmichael transferred to Anderson? *A.* None whatever, so far as the records show, or as I know.

Q. Is this an enquiry from General Talcott, addressed to Mr.
435 Anderson on the 10th April, 1851? *A.* It is.

The letter here read as follows:

ORDNANCE DAPARTMENT,
Washington, April 10th, 1851.

JOSEPH R. ANDERSON, ESQ., *Washington, D. C.*

Sir,—As Col. Huger is absent from his post on leave, and I desire early information in regard to the arrangement, whereby shot and shells are being supplied from the Tredegar Works to Fort Monroe Arsenal, I have to request such information from you.
436 You will oblige me by a statement of the nature of the arrangement, its date, what orders have been given under it, what deliveries have been made, and what are the prices agreed on for each kind of shot and shells; also any other terms and conditions in regard to deliveries.

Respectfully your ob't serv't,
G. TALCOTT,
Bt. Brig. Genl., Col. of Ordnance.

Q. On what day was Mr. Green's letter of the 5th April refer-
437 red to your office? *A.* It was received on the 10th April, and I think was referred there on that day, before that letter just read was written to Mr. Anderson; earlier in the day.

Q. What is the regulation allowance of ammunition to be expended in the year, by the garrison at Fort Monroe, in experiments and artillery practice? *A.* About 100 rounds per company; there are about three companies there now.

Q. Had the commander of the arsenal heretofore procured shot and shells for his own practice and experiments before the 6th November, 1850? *A.* He had procured them in small quantities.

438 *Q.* Under what authority? *A.* He was in the habit of putting in his quarterly estimates, a certain amount to be expended for purposes of experiments, and that amount was remitted, on the approval of his estimates by the Ordnance Office, and its requisition on the War Department for the funds. I recollect some orders to him, specially directing him to make certain experi

ments; but he always had authority for these experiments, either
general, in the way I have stated, or special, as on the occasions 439
mentioned, when he was instructed to make particular experiments.

Q. You have said, that when you drew up from the records of the Ordinance Office, the report to the Secretary of War, dated 22d January, that you had no knowledge of any other contract chargeable on the appropriations for armament of fortifications and for ordnance and ordnance stores and supplies, other than those stated in that report; and you stated at another time that you knew, in the latter part of December, that Dr. Carmichael had received a large order from Col. Huger, which was in the
hands of Mr. Anderson; do you desire to be understood that you did 440
not understand this order to be a contract, or how do you desire your testimony in these matters to be understood? *A.* I prepared the report of the 22d January from the records of the Ordnance Office solely; I then had no idea that the Secretary's call for information, had any reference to the Carmichael transaction, but supposed it to relate to the state of the appropriations exclusively. Congress was in session at that time, and there was much talk about the large amount of army estimates. The committee of ways and means were understood to be scrutinizing those estimates, with a view to their reduction, and I thought the Secretary wanted the information for that committee; hence that part 441
of the letter over and above the answer to the literal and strict call for information. I then knew of General Talcott's order to Col. Huger, I knew of Huger's order to Carmichael, from the copy which had been sent me by Mr. Anderson, and of Carmichael's sale to Mr. Anderson. But I firmly believed that the order in the hands of Mr. Anderson was suspended as to execution, that it constituted no outstanding charge or any appropriation, and that it was at most but a claim on the part of Anderson for a contract, which claim was to be recognized or rejected thereafter. I had received a letter from Mr. Anderson
in the latter part of December, inquiring if I knew Col. Huger's 442
reasons for declining to allow him to fulfil the order, and I had been assured by General Talcott that there was no outstanding contract for shot. I remained under this firm conviction, until the letter from Mr. Green was received at the Ordnance Office on the 10th April. I always supposed, and frequently mentioned to General Talcott, that Col. Huger had, in my opinion, exceeded his instructions of the the 6th November, in giving the order to Dr. Carmichael, and that his conduct in giving that order, was to me totally inexplicable. These instructions of the 6th Nov.
were the only ones that I knew had been given, and I did not 443
learn until the receipt of the Secretary of War's letter of the 1st May, any thing whatever of the interviews and conversations between General Talcott and the Secretary, in relation to the Carmichael transaction. •The report of the War Department of the

27th January was prepared by me, on information from General
Talcott, that there was no contract outstanding for shot. It then
first occurred to me that the Secretary might be referring to the
order to Col. Huger. I mentioned this to General Talcott, and
suggested to him the sending of a copy of that order, although not
444 called for, desiring to answer the call both as to its letter and its
spirit.

Q. What did General Talcott say when you told him that
Col. Huger had exceeded instructions? *A.* On the particular
occasion which I refer to, which was when I read Anderson's
letter, in the latter part of December, I dont think that Gen. Talcott said any thing in answer to what I said about Huger's exceeding instructions. But on other occasions, when I told him that
I could not account for Huger's strange conduct, in giving such
an order, unless something else had passed between them, he
445 assured me that nothing else had passed.

No cross-examination by defence.

Brevet Col. B. Huger, a witness on the part of the prosecution recalled.

Direct examination by Judge Advocate.

Q. Is that your letter of the 5th Nov. to General Talcott? *A.* Yes sir, (letter of witness of 5th November recorded page 181, here shown to witness.)

Q. What answer, if any, dated the 6th Nov., as thereon endorsed, did you receive to it? *A.* I received in answer to this letter,
446 the letter brought by the hands of Doctor Carmichael, dated the
6th November, 1850, which is already on your record, and recited
in the charges, and that is the only answer.

Q. You speak in the letter of the 5th November, of a note from General Talcott to you dated 1st Nov. Have you that note, if so, produce it, and if not, tell its contents. *A.* I have not the note. I received it on the morning of the 5th Nov, by the hands of Dr. Carmichael, it was marked private, and its contents were to this effect.

My dear Col.—Do you want any shot or shells for Fort Mon-
447 roe, if so, what quantity and calibres? That was the whole of
it, and this letter was my reply.

Q. How had you, before the letter of the 6th Nov., 1850, from General Talcott, procured shot and shells for experiments and artillery practice? *A.* Generally if not always on my own order, as I considered I had a standing authority to that effect. When I had orders to make experiments I understood the order to authorize me to get the necessary projectiles, when I made experiments without special instructions, I considered I had general authority.

448 *Q.* Did General Talcott when you informed him here, in Nov.
1850, of the order you had given Carmichael, instruct you, that
you had misconstrued his letter of the 6th November, and that
that letter was intended to convey to you only authority to pro-

cure projectiles for experiments and artillery practice? *A.* He
made no such statement to me at the time I was here in Nov.
when I answered the letters to Kemble and Anderson. But I 449
have heard him often say at different times since, that he presumed
in giving that order to Carmichael, that I would only give him
such small amounts as I wanted for experiments.

Q. When were these last times when he so said? *A.* I did not see General Talcott again after I left here in November, until I came here in April, under an order from the Secretary of War.

Q. Was this the time when the Secretary sent for you to enquire of you in this matter? *A.* Yes sir, when I was then here I heard General Talcott mention this, and since.

Cross examination by defence: 450

Q. After you had repudiated the transfer by Carmichael to Anderson of your order to the former, was not the order of the 6th Nov. available for procuring shot and shells for experiments, up to the date when the Secretary of War forbid the reception of shot and shells from any quarter? *A.* Of course the order was available to me until revoked by the authority that gave it.

And the prosecution here closed.

William L. Marcy, a witness on the part of the defence, being sworn in due form of law, testified as follows:

Q. Please to state to the court at what period, and for what 451
length of time you held the office of Secretary of War, and
whether, during your administration of that department, General
Talcott was the chief of the Ordnance Bureau? *A.* I was Secretary of War for 4 years, from March 1845 to March 1849; during the whole of that time General Talcott was at the head of
the Ordnance Bureau; part of the time the acting head, and part
of the time the actual head.

Q. Please to state what was the practical construction of, and
usage under the Ordnance Regulations, in regard to the procuring
of supplies during your administration, as to the distinction be- 452
tween contracts and open purchases, and whether these last, to
such reasonable extent as might be from time to time necessary,
were not ordinarily made by the bureau without the special *previous* authority of the Department? *A.* In relation to contracts,
I think there were very few written contracts, or none in the
form specified in this article 232, while I was in the War Department; I think most of the supplies were obtained by open purchases; there were some old contracts that were enlarged, extended, having reference to the terms of the original contracts;
whether they were in writing I am unable to say; they were 453
made before I went into the office; open purchases were frequently
made by the chief of the Ordnance Department, without previous
orders from the Secretary of War; there was frequent intercourse
between the head of the bureau and the Secretary, and questions
in regard to supplies frequently brought up for consultation and
advisement, as to the supplies and the price, and after such con-

sideration, I frequently expressed my consent that he should go on and procure the supplies; I can not say I gave express orders; the head of the bureau was required to make every year, estimates
454 of what was required for his branch of the service; when he submitted these, I required explanations; sometimes the estimates were reduced or cut down, but those which I thought required for the public service, I adopted; these were submitted to Congress, and the appropriations made, of course, sometimes with modifications, and then the bureau went on without my requiring him to apply to me for any further particular directions, and expended the money; I suppose the head of the bureau considered that he had my consent, as I had approved the estimates; I do not mean to say that I did not expect to be consulted, as the appropriations were sometimes very general.

355 As to the distinction between contracts and open purchases, I suppose that a contract under this article (132) must be in writing, and in three parts; I believe none such were ever made while I was in the War Department; I don't recollect of any.

Q. Was not the term open purchase understood and acted upon as applicable to orders for articles to be thereafter made and delivered, as well to articles already in existence? *A.* Yes.

Q. Please to state whether the affairs of the Ordnance Bureau were of magnitude and importance during your administration,
456 and whether they were managed with fidelity or otherwise by Gen. Talcott? *A.* They were of very great importance in their character and extent, particularly during the war; I certainly thought they were managed with fidelity by Gen. Talcott.

Cross examination:

Q. Was the question ever raised, and your attention ever called, while you were in the War Department (that you now recollect), to the distinction conveyed in the laws and regulations between contracts and open purchases, and the discussions of that question by two of the Attorney Generals? *A.* I am not aware that I knew of any discussion of that subject by the At-
457 torney General; but I did know that there were different classes of contracts; that the laws had imposed different modes of making contracts.

Q. If no written contracts in three parts were made during your administration, were not the engagements made to furnish supplies ordinarily called contracts? *A.* I believe they were in common parlance, and without reference to the distinction made by the article. They were called contracts or purchases in common parlance indiscriminately in most instances.

The defence here offered an extract from a letter from the Hon. John C. Spencer, Ex-Secretary of War, to General Talcott,
458 and stated that Mr. Spencer had been summoned as a witness on the part of the defence, and had not been able, on account of ill health, to come. It was read as follows:

ALBANY, June 28, 1851.

"While I was in the department, the difference between an
open purchase and a contract was recognized and constantly 459
acted upon; that the strict contract system was believed to be
entirely inapplicable to many articles necessary for the ordnance
service, and that orders for articles, such as cannon and shot,
were, according to my belief, given long ahead of their manufacture at specified prices; and that these were never regarded as contracts because, &c. &c. &c."

The Judge Advocate said he admitted the statement as evidence from Mr. Spencer to the facts stated; but he could not admit in evidence his reasonings upon the law.

The defence here closed. General Talcott asked time until 460
next Monday, at 1 o'clock, to prepare a written address to the
court, which application the court granted, and then adjourned
to meet on Monday at 1 o'clock.

WASHINGTON, Monday, July 7th, 1851.

The court met pursuant to adjournment. Present, all the
members and Judge Advocate, when the proceedings of the last
day were read over, and General Talcott laid before the court 461
the address in writing which is appended to this record, which
address was then read to the court by the counsel for the defence,
J. M. Carlisle, Esq.

The Judge Advocate then stated that he submitted the case to the court without argument on the part of the prosecution.

Whereupon the court was cleared and, in closed session, with mature deliberation upon all the evidence, pronounced the following findings and sentence:

That the accused, Brevet Brigadier General George Talcott,
Colonel of the Ordnance Department, is *guilty* of the specifica- 462
tion to the first charge.

That he is *guilty* of the first charge.

That he is *guilty* of the specification to the second charge.

That he is *guilty* of the second charge.

That he is *guilty* of the first specification to the third charge, except the words therein, "*and had previously reported to the Secretary of War.*"

That he is *not guilty* of the second specification to the third charge.

That he is *guilty* of the third specification to the third charge. 463

That he is *guilty* of the fourth specification to the third charge.

That he is *guilty* of the fifth specification to the third charge.

That he is *guilty* of the sixth specification to the third charge.

That he is *guilty* of the seventh specification to the third charge.

And that he is *guilty* of the third charge.

And the court sentence him, Brevet Brigadier General George
464 Talcott, Colonel of the Ordnance Department, *to be dismissed the service.*

(Signed) D. E. TWIGGS,
Bt. Maj. Gen. U. S. A., President Court.

(Signed) J. F. LEE, *Judge Advocate.*

The court adjourned to meet to-morrow at 10 o'clock.

---

465 Tuesday, 10 o'clock, July 8, 1851.

The court met pursuant to adjournment. Present, all the members and Judge Advocate. The record of yesterday was read and approved, and the court adjourned without day.

(Signed) D. E. TWIGGS,
Bt. Maj. Gen. U. S. A., Pres't Court.

(Signed) J. F. LEE, *Judge Advocate.*

---

466 Under the circumstances of the case, the undersigned, member of the General Court Martial, respectfully recommends the accused to the clemency of the Executive.

(Signed) J. J. ABERT,
Colonel Corps Topographical Engineers.

EXECUTIVE MANSION, July 8, 1851.

The foregoing proceedings of a court martial, for the trial of
Brevet Brigadier General George Talcott, having been laid before
467 me, and having been by me duly examined and considered, I
hereby confirm the same.

(Signed) MILLARD FILLMORE.

GEN. TALCOTT'S DEFENCE.

Mr. President and Gentlemen of the Court:

This occasion, I doubt not, is to you, as it is to me, full of interest and solemnity. If I feel the unspeakable value of an 468
honorable name, so likewise do you. If I have heretofore worn
mine with an honest pride, so has each one of you. And though
it is my fortune and not yours, to be summoned now to defend
my right to this priceless possession, after having borne it unques-
tioned up the hill of life, across the narrow table land which
lies at its summit, and far downward in the path that leads to the
vale below; yet do I feel and know that this contest has stirred
in the breasts of my judges something of that earnestness which
fills my own. 469

It is not enough that I have been sustained by the consciousness of my own rectitude; that I have looked forward from the
beginning with unshaken confidence to the issue of this investigation; that I now count upon your justice to accord to me a full
and ready acquittal of the charges laid against me. There are
wounds which it is not in the power of human justice wholly
to heal. Such a wound is this arraignment before my peers, and
in the face of my country, to answer to a charge of the detestable
crime of willful and deliberate falsehood; a crime which poisons
the very spring and fountain of common honesty.

It is this which gives to these charges their envenomed and 470
immedicable sting. It is to this that I shall most earnestly address myself in these remarks; and if I shall fail to sustain
myself, not merely against the technical specifications to which
I am to answer, but against all doubt, and all suspicions, then,
indeed, will I have failed to attain the object which, at this moment, I desire above all earthly things.

I am not insensible to the gravity of the other charges preferred
against me; but you will require no word of explanation from
me to make you comprehend how insignificant they appear to me
in comparison with that which not only imputes to me a military
offence, but impeaches my personal honor as a private gentleman. It is my purpose to examine them each, and to rely upon
no merely technical defence as to either. 471

For the result of this trial it would be sufficient for me to show
that neither of these charges has been clearly and specifically
established, by irresistible proof, beyond all reasonable doubt.

Showing this much and no more, I should be entitled to an
acquittal. But I desire that this paper, side by side with the
accusations against me, shall exhibit their complete refutation,
not in form only, but in substance and spirit; and to this end it
472 is necessary that, even at the risk of being tedious, I should review in detail every act and declaration which has been arrayed
against me, from the beginning to the end of the period covered
by the charges and specifications. I am not unconscious that,
upon such a review, it is possible that very different conclusions
may be reached by different minds, though actuated perhaps by
the same desire to discover the truth. In my commentary, therefore, upon the extraordinary inferences which have been drawn,
in a high quarter, from circumstances which, to say the least of
them, are surely not irreconcileable with pure and innocent intentions, I shall be far from imputing any malicious or unfair
motive to the mind which has colored them with the dark hues
473 of infamy and guilt. I am not now to learn for the first time
that there is a disease which sometimes, though rarely, infects
the most honorable minds, but usually by contact with baser
spirits; a disease of jaundiced suspicion, which no sooner is communicated to its subject than "trifles light as air" become "confirmation strong as proofs from holy writ." You, sir, and
gentlemen, will approach this subject, I am sure, with no such
foregone conclusions. You will approach it remembering that
your inquiry is for the motive and intention of a man whose life
474 has not been spent in holes and corners, but who has walked
openly, and in the light of day, upon the same theatre which
your own footsteps have marked with such distinguished honor;
a man who, if he has in these transactions entered the dark and
tortuous path of infamy, has, without any imaginable motive,
suddenly turned his back upon the object of his pursuit through
life, and thrown away in the merest wantonness, a treasure for
which that life would have been too small a sacrifice.

And here, better than elsewhere, I may invite your attention
to that which can not be disputed, and which, at the outset, pours
475 a flood of light over the whole field of investigation. I mean
the total absence of the imputation, or fair suspicion, of any motive for the commission of the offences which are charged against
me.

I am charged with violating the 132d article of the Ordnance
Regulations, in approving and allowing a contract, in relation to
which not only is it not charged that I had any interest, but upon
the state of facts, as you will see when you come to apply them
to this question, utterly repugnant to and irreconcileable with
any such interest.

476 I am charged with willful disobedience of orders and instructions from the Secretary of War, when, upon the same state of
facts, no conceivable motives can be assigned for such disobedience.

And finally, I am charged with repeated falsehoods and false

reports, when not only the same entire absence of motive is apparent, but when the veriest dolt on the earth must have seen that
imminent, inevitable detection stood ready at his right hand, and 477
open shame was staring him in the face.

Am I that monstrous anomaly in human nature, so to act as to outrage every rule of human action? Or are you not to try me as a MAN—to examine my conduct, holding those great rules and springs of action as applicable to me as to yourselves. So manifest and so impossible to be passed over does this great gap in the case appear to me, that I can not but suppose that those who framed these charges, and who considered them worthy of your attention, must have been helped across it by the unworthy suspicions of some of those mysterious personages "*not connected
in any manner with the department*," who, it would appear by the 478
testimony of the Hon. Secretary, have stood ready even during the progress of my trial, to make suggestions to him that other facts existed than those which his vigilance had suspected, and that those facts were of importance to be searched for and found. I refer particularly to the letter of Col. Huger, *discovered* in its regular place among the files of the department upon the suggestion of "*a gentleman not in any manner connected with the department.*"

I proceed now to an examination of the charges and specifications in detail.

CHARGE I. 479

Violation of the 132d Article of the Regulations for the Government of the Ordnance Department.

Upon this charge I remark first, that it alleges that I have violated an article which expressly, and by its terms, purports to regulate the conduct of officers and agents of the Ordnance Department, inferior to the chief of that department, and which neither by its terms, nor by any fair implication, lays any injunction upon the chief of the department, or prescribes any rule for his conduct. If this be so, it will require no argument to show
that it is not legally or logically possible that I can be guilty of 480
a violation of that article, upon any state of facts whatever. A man can not violate a law which does not prescribe a rule of conduct for him; for, as to him, it is no law. The language of the article is as follows:

"No contract for the service of the Ordnance Department shall be made by any officer or agent thereof, *except by special authority from the Chief of the Ordnance Department*, sanctioned by the Secretary of War: and all officers or agents making contracts shall strictly observe the provisions of the laws on that
subject. (See appendix No. 2.) Contracts shall be made in 481
triplicate, one of which *shall be forwarded* TO THE CHIEF OF THE ORDNANCE DEPARTMENT, at the date of the contract, that it may

be deposited in the office of the Second Comptroller within ninety days thereafter, as the law directs."

482 The question is *to whom* is this command addressed? The *persons to whom* it is addressed are directed before making any contract, to *obtain my special* authority.

Can I then be *one of those persons?* Not unless the absurd construction be given to the article, that before making a contract I shall take care to *get my own special authority* to do so? The persons to whom it is addressed are commanded to *forward* one copy of the contract *to me.* Can I myself, then, be one of those persons? Not unless the regulation has imposed upon me the duty of inventing some mode by which I can "forward" one copy of the contract to myself.

483 If, therefore, I had made a contract, and if the making of the contract was unauthorized and improper, surely nothing can be clearer than that my offence, if any, is not a violation of the 132d article; and consequently, that I am not guilty of the first charge.

But, in fact and in law, I made no contract. Not only did I make no contract in the sense, and within the terms of that article, but I made no contract in law or in fact, in any sense whatever, general or special. Nor, indeed, does the specification under this charge impute to me that I made a contract. For,
484 first, it distinctly charges that a contract was made by *Colonel Huger*, under the authority of my letter of the 6th November, (of which I shall speak hereafter); then, *that I, fifteen* days afterwards, being informed of this, and "did allow and approve THE ACT *of the said Huger*," and concludes as follows: "THEREBY *permitting and sanctioning* a contract, &c." So that, the charge being that *I* made a contract, the specification in support of it sums up all the facts—with a "THEREBY"—in a totally different offence, to wit: the subsequent approval of a contract made by another.

485 But, in point of fact, as I shall show you, there was not either prior authority or subsequent assent by me.

1st. As to previous authority. The specification sets out *the contract and the supposed authority.* Can it be necessary to do more than to collate these two written papers, and side by side to compare them, in order to decide at once that *that order* is no authority for *that contract?*

No one can have read them without expecting that if the making of that contract was to be charged to me, some other or further authority would be proven than what is contained in that
486 letter. Even the Secretary of War, to whom a copy of it was communicated in my report of the 27th of January, did not so understand it. In his testimony on that point he says: "*This answer*, (viz. the Report of the 27th January, enclosing a copy of the order of the 6th of November,) being PERFECTLY SATISFACTORY, *I ceased to think on the subject until my attention was again*

called to it a short time after, by Mr. Green AGAIN *mentioning the shot being made at the works at Richmond, when it occurred to me* 487
THAT POSSIBLY *Colonel Huger might be making shot under that order of the 6th of November.*"

From this testimony of the Secretary of War himself two things result conclusively, viz: 1st. That the Secretary of War, who, be it remembered, had been previously informed on two distinct occasions, by Mr. Thomas Green, that "the *Tredegar works had a large contract for shot for the War Department*," and that "a large quantity of shot was making at the Tredegar works in Richmond, owned by Mr. J. R. Anderson; and that a considerable quantity was piled up in the foundry yard, or somewhere about the foundry;" and who had his suspicions aroused, 488
and his mind turned directly to the investigation of this very point, received from me, and read, an official copy of that letter of the 6th of November, without imagining that it could be construed as authority for the alleged contract, or could even tend to render it probable that the information he had received *had any foundation* whatever until some time afterwards, when, with the aid of Mr. Thomas Green, "*it occurred to him that* POSSIBLY *Colonel Huger might be making shot under that order.* And secondly, that whereas it is now charged against me that the authority assumed in that order was usurped in violation of the regulations because not sanctioned by the Secretary of War, the Secretary himself has here testified before you, on oath, that 489
my report communicating to him that I had issued such an order, and transcribing the order word for word, and letter for letter, was by him considered "PERFECTLY SATISFACTORY," and that he "*ceased to think upon the subject. How could this be if he did not understand*, as I did, that *I had the authority to issue that order?* If any *sanction of his*, previous or subsequent, express or implied, were necessary, has he not here on oath placed it upon your record in the declaration that the report communicating that order was "*perfectly satisfactory*" and that he "*ceased to think on the subject.*"

Hear also what is said by Capt. Maynadier, the principal assist- 490
ant of the bureau, and a witness for the prosecution, not on his cross-examination, but while in the hands of the learned and gallant Judge Advocate. He says: "I always supposed and frequently mentioned to General Talcott, my firm belief that Colonel Huger had *exceeded his instructions*, in giving the order to Dr. Carmichael; and that his conduct in giving that order was to me totally inexplicable;" this, when he was familiar with every word in the order of the 6th of November. Need more be said or recapitulated to show that the contract, if *any contract was made*, was not in *pursuance of the letter of the 6th of November?* and that that letter, according *to its fair and natural import*, was, 491
in the judgment of the *Secretary of War* himself, *clearly within my official* competency, and "*perfectly satisfactory to him.*"

492 The question, then, remains, was that order the sole authority
given by me to Colonel Huger? Let him answer it himself.

I put the question to him roundly and distinctly: "Had you
any further or other authority from General Talcott in reference
to the procuring of shot or shells than the order of the 6th November,
recited on the charges?" His answer is simply and
distinctly, "No." Not only is this testimony entitled to be
received as conclusive, on account of the character and standing
of the witness, his position here as a witness for the prosecution,
and the powerful inducements, if it were possible for him to
swerve from the truth, all operating to draw from him his own
493 justification for the order given by him; but there is no particle
of evidence upon the record giving you the slightest ground for
depriving it of one atom of its controlling and overwhelming
weight upon this part of the case. When I inquired of him in
an unofficial letter—"*Do you want any shot or shells for Fort
Monroe? if so, what quantity and calibre?*" his reply of the 5th
giving me no information to enable *me* to cause such purchases
to be made as I had supposed might be required, my letter of the
6th of November was written, departing in no degree from the
idea which I originally entertained, that purchases to a limited
extent might be necessary—not expressly or impliedly authorizing
or contemplating the complete armament of the Fort, or any
494 large supplies, or any thing like it; but plainly and clearly, in as
simple words as language affords, limiting his authority to procuring
them, *from* time to time, to a reasonable extent, if they could
be had on reasonable terms, and by open purchase only. *This,
my sole authority to Colonel Huger, and my sole reply to his letter,
was read and considered by the Secretary of War under the peculiar
circumstances already adverted to, and was regarded by him
as* "PERFECTLY SATISFACTORY."

It is not to be imputed to him that he did not know his duty;
that he was not acquainted with the limits of his own powers, and
of mine. And if that order contained anything more than I had
the clear right to do, it is impossible that it could have been
495 "*perfectly satisfactory*" to him, or that he should have "ceased
to think" upon a subject which had brought officially and directly
to his notice, the usurpation of power and the violation of law
by the head of one of the bureaux of the department confided to
his charge. If anything further were needed on this point, it is
to be found in the order issued by the Secretary nearly three
months after my letter of the 6th of Nov., which directs that the
heads of bureaux of the department should not *thereafter* "make
or authorize any contracts for supplies, or for arms and munitions
of war to be furnished, or for services to be performed,
without previously submitting such contracts or propositions to
the Secretary of War," an order which was perfectly nugatory
496 and unmeaning, unless indeed such previous sanction had not
been required theretofore in procuring supplies to an amount ex-

ceeding two thousand dollars. The Secretary says that he was
informed (and it is to be presumed through the proper official
channels) that it had been the practice of the Ordnance Bureau 497
not to require such previous sanction in cases exceeding two
thousand dollars. The 132d regulation itself, if by a violent
construction it can be held applicable to the chief of the bureau,
does not express whether the sanction is to be previous or subsequent. If, therefore, such practice did exist, it was a practical
construction of the article, tacitly approved, and a sufficient justification of an act done in accordance with it.

To this point also is the testimony of Governor Marcy; nor
was there any subsequent approval by me of the order given to 498
Dr. Carmichael. I shall have occasion presently to review my
conduct in this respect, with reference to the last charge. At
present I content myself with saying that no such approval has
been proven. On the contrary, Colonel Huger, who alone could
prove it, and had every motive to do so if it had taken place, has
testified that I expressed surprise at the amount of the order he
had given, when it was first made known to me, and when, as I
shall demonstrate at the same moment, all the necessary steps
were taken to make that order, or purchase, or contract, or by
whatsoever name it may be described, as completely dead, and
null, and void, as if it had never for one moment existed. 499

And when afterwards he is pressed by the Judge Advocate on
this point, and his attention called directly to the same period
by the following question:

Q. "You say on the cross examination, and in answer to the
question next before the last, that you had no further authority
from General Talcott in reference to the procuring shot and
shells than the order of the 6th November; do you mean that
you received no authority from him personally here in November, 1850?" He answers, "*None whatever*, unless his approval
of my letters to Anderson by Capt. Stone, and mine to Kemble,
be considered as such, *which I do not*." There was, then, neither
prior authority for, nor subsequent approval of, the order to 500
Carmichael set out in the specification.

Charge II.

The *Second Charge* I shall despatch in a few words. I venture to affirm that no precedent could have been found for a
charge and specification of "*willful disobedience of orders and
instructions*," in which it is not charged specifically and distinctly
that orders and instructions were in fact given, and what those
orders and instructions were. Yet such are this charge and
specification; not indeed from any fault of the Judge Advocate,
for his learning and ability in such matters would enable him to 501
wear the gown of the barrister with equal ease and grace as he
now wears the epaulets of the soldier, and the pen is as familiar to him as the sword, but because in fact no such orders
or instructions were given, and none have been attempted to be

proven. Indeed the honorable Secretary has virtually aban-
doned and renounced this charge upon his examination here,
502 when he said that in stating at the interview with Mr. Anderson in April last, that "the question was whether an order of
the department had been disobeyed," he supposed that the shot
had been made subsequently to the regulation of the 29th of
January, and that the order referred to was *that order* only. If
he had given an order, or anything like an order, in reference to
Dr. Carmichael specifically, it is not possible that his mind would
have passed over that order, with which the precise matter was
directly connected, to refer the disobedience to a general regulation made long after the order of the 6th November, which had
503 been two months before submitted to him.

But I aver that there was nothing said or done by the Secretary at the interview with Dr. Carmichael in November, which implied or could lead me to imagine that he meant to forbid the making of any purchase, or ordering of any supplies from that person.

The matter before him gave no occasion for the expression of
his wishes on that subject. It was a distinct specific application
by Dr. Carmichael for a certain specified contract, in redemption
of the pledge which he alleged he had received. I aver that I
heard nothing of any other application or any other pretension
504 by Dr. Carmichael treated of or decided by the Secretary. His
decision was, that there had been no recognition of this pledge,
and that he would not recognize it. I certainly so understood it,
and so referred to it, as he himself has testified, when next I
met him. But in order that there might be no doubt upon the
subject, I put the question distinctly, whether any other application than the one specified was in fact made, to which he gave
no other answer than by recapitulating the arguments and per-
suasive suggestions used by Dr. Carmichael in support of his
pretensions. And when asked if he had even told Dr. Carmi-
505 chael in my presence, that the department was not in want of
any shot, he can only give his impressions, qualified with the
declaration that he "*would not be positive.*" Is this the evidence upon which an officer is to be convicted of "willful disobedience of orders and instructions?"

Charge III.

I pass now to the remaining charge. The first specification
has been fully answered in what has been already said. So likewise has the second, except as to the allegation that I knew that
506 Dr. Carmichael was "not in a capacity to execute the said contract otherwise than through a sale or assignment." To this
allegation, it is a sufficient answer that no title or proof has been
offered to sustain it; but on the contrary, my conduct in refusing to recognize the transfer refutes it. If I am not deluded in
my firm confidence that I am to be tried here at least not by
suspicions, but by proofs, it is waste of time to say more. The

third specification presents in a solid body the whole array of
falsehoods and deceptions charged against me; and the fourth,
fifth, sixth and seventh, while they have the appearance of re- 507
enforcing it, are but reproductions of the same array in several
detachments. I shall treat them together. There is still another of these black and hateful offences, not indeed specifically laid in the charges, but reserved for the testimony, and performing the preparatory office of introducing me to you at the threshhold of this transaction, under a dark cloud of guilt; not speaking, but in silence uttering a lie, and by my presence maintaining the unfounded pretensions of another. I allude to the circumstances detailed by the Hon. Secretary touching my introduction of Dr. Carmichael to him about the end of October, or
beginning of November; a detail which I think you must have 508
heard, without imagining that any human being could see more in it than common courtesy and official duty combined, until the further testimony of the witness disclosed to you that he indeed thought "'twas strange—'twas passing strange—'twas wonderful."

That it really and truly made upon his mind the impression he has communicated to you, no one can doubt; but that it can similarly affect any mind not in some mode prepared to think the worst of me, I can not apprehend. That the chief of a bureau could not venture to accede to the request of a person 509
whose social position itself entitles him to it, to introduce him to the Secretary in order that he might prefer a claim (against which the bureau had already decided of record) without incurring the obligation to interrupt the conversation between them by flat denials of the pretensions of the claimant, at the risk of having his own fidelity suspected, certainly never occurred to me. Still less that such suspicion could arise when, as the Secretary himself has stated, I held the papers, and all the papers necessary to show the whole truth of the case, in my hand before him, in such manner as naturally to lead him to ask at the
proper moment, "General, are those the papers?" Nor can I 510
suppose it to be material whether I instantly sprang to my feet and tendered the papers to him, or whether that question being answered in the affirmative, he requested me to hand them to him. This conduct, however, the Hon. Secretary has again and again repeated and reiterated he thought "singular" and "surprising" conduct, for which "he could not account." And being asked by a member of the court whether there was anything in the circumstances authorizing him to suppose that I would not have expressed my opinion if he had not himself reached the
same conclusion upon a perusal of the papers, he answered not 511
by specifying any such circumstance, nor by expressly admitting that no such circumstance existed; but as follows:

"*The reason why my surprise at General Talcott's silence* when Dr. Carmichael asserted that there had been a written recogni-

tion of the contract by Mr. Crawford was *increased by his remarking the next day, or a day or two afterwards, that I was right,* was that I had supposed *it possible that Gen. Talcott might* have
512 agreed with Dr. Carmichael in supposing that the letter of Mr. Crawford amounted to a recognition; but when he said he agreed with me that there was no such recognition, my surprise at his silence *increased,* because I did not know how to account for it." From this it would seem either that the Secretary regarded that paper as really susceptible of the constructions, or that he was vascillating between two opinions, that I was either a knave or a fool. If I have seemed to dwell too long upon this point, I beg the court to remember that in order to a just decision upon the remaining accusations, which depend upon conversations between two persons, one of whom is the sole witness, and the other the
513 accused, whose statement is no evidence, it is of the first importance that you should as far as possible enter into the minds of the persons respectively, and discover with what preoccupations and upon what foregone conclusions they severally spoke. The question is not what words were uttered, but with what intent and meaning they were uttered. Without enlarging upon this suggestion, I proceed now to shew what ideas occupied my own mind on the various occasions referred to in these specifications; as to which I remark in passing, that if I have correctly noted the testimony, it falls short by one of the number of conversations alleged. It is abundantly clear upon the record, that from
514 the date of my letter to Col. Huger of 6th of Novmber, up to the receipt of the letter from Mr. Kemble, I knew nothing of the order given to Dr. Carmichael, nor had I any reason to imagine that *any such* order had been given.

That upon the receipt of that letter, I referred it to Col. Huger, then in Washington on special duty, with directions to reply to it, as I knew nothing of the facts to which it related; that he then first communicated to me what he had done upon the supposed authority of my order.

That I "expressed my surprise" at what he had done; that I
515 also, in reference of the offer of the order for sale, told him that "the Secretary of War would be incensed, and justly so if an order for supplies should be hawked about the market."

That I refused my assent to any transfer of it; that he accordingly repudiated the proposed transfer to Mr. Kemble, and the subsequent transfer to Mr. Anderson; all of which occurred within twenty days from the date of the letter to Col. Huger, and promptly after I was informed of what he had done under it. It was now clear that Dr. Carmichael's representations to Col. Huger were unfounded, and could not be fulfilled by him, and
516 that in his own hands, the order, if it ever had validity, was null and void. From the date of his assignment to Mr. Anderson, certainly he had no shadow of right to claim the execution of the order so indiscreetly given to him, even if at any time that

order constituted a contract, or imposed any binding obligation
upon the department. It was equally clear and indisputable,
that by the express terms of the regulation No. 133, if any rights 517
whatever had vested in him as a contractor, they could not "be
transferred to any other person or persons" under any circumstances whatever. Was there then any contract outstanding for
shot for the Ordnance Department? Who except Mr. Anderson
affirms that there was? Does the prosecution, now that the case
is known, assert or admit that there was? Does the Secretary
of War assert or admit that there was? If he does, by what
right, moral or legal, does he, when made acquainted with all
the facts, prevent the execution of that contract? As I asserted
when in entire ignorance of the fact that any shot had been 518
made, or any attempt to induce Colonel Huger to recede from
the position which he had taken under my directions, so I now
assert and maintain that no such contract existed. Not only
was there never any contract, in the sense of the Ordnance Regulations, or in any strict legal sense, but the particular purchase
attempted by Col. Huger, in misapprehension of the terms of
my authorization of the 6th of November, had fortunately entirely
failed so as to leave no pretence whatever of any obligation upon
the government to accept a performance of the order so impro-
vidently given to Dr. Carmichael. And this state of things, be it 519
remembered, was brought to my knowledge simultaneously with
the first information of the fact that Col. Huger had given that
order. Am I wrong in these conclusions, or either of them? You
have before you, in the shape of testimony as to the usage of the
department, the incidental expression of the opinion of one of the
most distinguished jurists in the country, the Hon. John C. Spencer.
When speaking of the usage, he says, "*orders* for articles, such
as cannon and shot, were, according to my belief, given long
ahead of their manufacture, at specified prices; and these were
never regarded as contracts, because a contract implies an obli- 520
gation on each side, the one to furnish, and the other to pay.
But an order for articles at a specified price, received by a party,
creates no obligation on his part to furnish the articles. Nor
indeed does it create an *obligation* on the party giving the order,
for there is no consideration for it, and it is revocable at any
time."

This is not the tribunal or the occasion to enlarge upon this
point, nor is it necessary to do more than to refer to it in passing.
Certainly there can be no two opinions upon the point that an
order to Dr. Carmichael, given with the distinct agreement that 521
it should be executed at a certain fonndry, and under a specified
superintendence (the freight from that certain foundry being calculated and turned into the price), could not be binding in morals
or in law when transferred to *another* person, to be executed at
another foundry, and under different *superintendence*; above all
when, as appears in the case from the statement of Captain

Stone, who at the request of Col. Huger arranged the details
with Dr. Carmichael, his attention was at that very time called
522 to shot and shells received from the very foundry to which the
order was afterwards assigned, and the fact that they were not
fabricated satisfactorily remarked upon by Capt. Stone. This
last fact, though unknown to me at the time, is material as to
the fundamental assumption which lies at the bottom of all these
specifications, viz: that there was in truth an outstanding contract,
the existence of which I knew, and denied. Nor can it be
questioned that if Col. Huger's order in the first instance constituted
a contract, neither the proprietor of the Tredegar Works,
nor any other person, could acquire any rights whatsoever by a
523 transfer or assignment of it, by whatsoever contrivance or indirection
the *form of an* assignment might be suppressed or evaded.
Col. Huger in his written deposition before the Secretary of War,
here given in evidence by the prosecution, states the point clearly
and correctly. "Witness directed Capt. Stone to return the
power of attorney to Mr. Anderson, and inform him that he considered
the power of attorney as in substance an assignment of
the order, and that Mr. Carmichael had no right to make such a
transfer, and that he, witness, would not recognize it."

An attempt has been made to show apparently, that such eva-
523 sion is countenanced and admitted at the treasury. Upon this
I have no farther commentary to make, than to say that if such
is the practice, it is a violation of the law, in letter and spirit,
and is a strange commentary upon the gravamen of one of those
specifications which alleges, as a disgraceful offence, that the
public service was "exposed *to the discredit* arising from the sale
of a public contract;" an offence which it would then seem the
government encourages and protects.

This, then, was the state of things, as made known to me in
the month of November, simultaneously with my first informa-
526 tion of Colonel Huger's misconstruction of the terms of my letter.
The order had become, to all intents and purposes, to affect
the department, a mere dead letter. I had no reason to believe,
or imagine, that any thing could be done, or would be attempted
under it. Being entirely satisfied that Colonel Huger had acted
as he has always done, with the best and purest intentions, and
with a view to the public service according to his judgment,
and that his mere error of judgment had resulted, and could result
in no injury to the government, it required a new quality to
be infused into my nature before I could for a moment think of
527 gratuitously involving him in any difficulty. Not only had I no
reason to suppose that anything had been done under the Carmichael
order, but so late as the end of December I had the most
satisfactory, positive evidence, that nothing had been done. I refer
to the correspondence between Mr. Anderson, and Captain
Maynadier, in which Mr. Anderson *complains that Colonel Huger
will not allow him to execute* this order, *inquires if Colonel Huger*

has any personal objection to him (Anderson,) and states the circumstances and reasons, which he supposed made such refusal inequitable. It must have been shortly after this, certainly before I had any reason to believe that the condition of things had 528
at all changed, that the Secretary made his first inquiry of me. In his testimony he does not detail explicitly what that inquiry was, or in what language it was expressed, though this is material, in order to understand the answer, and ascertain whether it was true, and to the point. But it may be *inferred* from what he says, viz: that he had been "informed *that the Tredegar works* HAD A LARGE CONTRACT FOR SHOT FOR THE WAR DEPARTMENT." That he sent for me and *informed me of it.* That I said "*it was a mistake; that no contract existed for shot, and that none was making at Richmond for the department.*"

I believe I have quoted his precise words. Not having access 529
to the record, I take them from the notes of counsel. In his written statement of the 1st May, addressed to me, also in evidence, he states my answer simply thus: "*You told me that it was an error; that no such contract existed.*"

Whether upon this occasion, or upon any of the subsequent occasions, I used language importing that, in point of fact, there was no shot making at the Tredegar works, not shot piled in the foundry, or shipped thence to Fort Monroe, can not be at all material; for such language could only have been uttered, and could only have been understood as denying that any shot was making, or made, or shipped *under a contract with or by authority of the* 530
Ordnance Department. It is not to be imagined that the Secretary of War could possibly have understood me as peremptorily denying, *here in Washington,* the existence of facts alleged *to be occurring in Richmond.*

All that I could deny, and all that was reasonable of him to inquire of me, was the allegation that any such facts existed by, or under the authority of the Ordnance Department. To have undertaken to go further than this, and positively to contradict physical facts, alledged to be occurring more than one hundred miles beyond my range of vision, would have been to offend his common sense, and to renounce my own. So the Secretary him- 531
self manifestly understood it; for upon Mr. Thomas Green's second report to him, he renews the investigation in writing, (as it now appears, though I had no intimation at the time that his purpose was other than a general one,) and the correspondence between the department and the bureau comprised in the six papers in your record, of dates from the 21st to the 27th of January, including a copy of the order to Colonel Huger, speaks for itself, and shows that the inquiry was simply as to existing contracts and charges upon the ordnance appropriations.

It can not escape your notice, as it has painfully forced itself 532
upon my own, that the course pursued by the Secretary, upon this second occasion, indicates too clearly that, from some source

or other, his mind had been so abused as to my character, that he
thought it necessary to approach me with generalities in order to
533 get at the truth. But I can not abandon the expectation that,
upon a review of the whole case, he too will see that he has unintentionally done me the greatest injustice. You have now the
key to all the specifications imputing falsehood to me.

In the mind of the Secretary was one thing; in mine, another.
If, in these repeated arraignments of me, I manifested, as he has
said, some impatience and heat, it was because I understood him
as again, and again, renewing an inquiry, which I had already
fully and truly answered, and in regard to which no single new
fact, or reason to believe a fact, had come to my knowledge from
the date of my first answer to the date of my declaration that
534 there was not a word of truth in Mr. Green's letter. Down to
the date of my interview with Mr. Anderson, who happened to
be in Washington when that letter was referred to me, I never
imagined that any act, or word of Colonel Huger had in any degree varied the condition of things in November, to wit: Dr.
Carmichael himself failing to comply with, and finally renouncing
and conveying to other hands, the improvident order which had
been given, and that transfer finally repudiated and rejected, and
no contract, or pretence of a contract, existing.

Nor do I mean to say that what had occurred, and was unknown
to me, did in fact vary the condition of things. It is not pretended that I knew any of these facts. The only circumstance
535 which appears to have been relied on as bearing upon this point
is, that Captain Mordecai mentioned to me casually that Colonel
Huger had requested him to send to Mr. Anderson a couple of
guages, and said he supposed there was no objection in sending
them; to which I answered, "I suppose not." But he himself
has testified that there was nothing either in Colonel Huger's request, or in what he said to me, inconsistent with the idea that
they were required to make a few shot for experiments, and that
he believed at the time that such was the object. I had no reason to believe, and did not believe, that it had any reference to
the execution of the order, the transfer of which had been dis-
536 tinctly and officially repudiated. My letter to Colonel Huger
remained, as he has stated, in force to authorize the procuring
of shot and shells for practice and experiment, and TO NO OTHER
EFFECT, as he was now fully advised of the mistake he had made.
Knowing it to be available for this object only, as I stated to the
Secretary of War, when asked whether Colonel Huger might
not be making shot under that order, I supposed the request for
the guages to relate to some purchase of that sort, and to nothing
else. I solemnly aver, that I understood the subsequent oral
537 interrogations of the Secretary, as I did the first, from the beginning to the end, as calling upon me to answer to a simple point,
to wit: the allegation that there was some contract, or arrangement, by which the Tredegar works, with my knowledge and

authority, were engaged in making a large quantity of shot for
the department. He fully sustains me in this upon his last cross 538
examination, when, in answer to a question presenting that view of the matter to him, he answers that in the inquiries which he made, he "*took it for granted*" that "the shot could not be making without my knowledge and authority." If this was so firmly rooted in his mind, can you doubt the assertion that he conveyed the same idea to me, and fixed my attention upon it as the substantial and only object of his inquiry? That I answered it truly, I appeal to this record to establish before the world. Take any other view of the case and you utterly stultify me; you must
believe that in an evil hour a double curse suddenly descended 539
on me—the loss of common honesty and common intellect. Not only must I, without motive, have become a liar, but I must have uttered falsehood while Truth stood over me scourge in hand. Could I know that Mr. Anderson, relying on acts and letters of Colonel Huger's, was engaged in executing an order, drawing largely upon his means and claiming the rights of a contractor, and yet dream that his mouth was to be closed, and his powerful motive of interest be stilled by my simple denial that such things existed? Must not a fool have seen that "that devil which will not down"—*interest*—the interest of a contractor whose invest-
ment, as well as his expected profits, were at stake—would tear 540
off the flimsy veil with which I had covered myself and leave me naked and cowering before the world? Is it creditable that I should have uttered falsehood after falsehood, while I beheld the figure of Mr. Anderson already advancing upon me, armed with bills, and estimates, and guages, and letters, and pointing triumphantly from these to a pyramid of shot at Fort Monroe to demand his money, and yet not make one step towards him—one faltering effort to stay the blow so sure to follow? And yet, not a word or sign from me to him, or from him to me, ever passed on this subject until he answered in person my letter of April, when directed to report to Mr. Thomas Green's leter; for although warned that nothing could be valid without my consent, 541
he made no approach to me, but doubtless "took it for granted" that, as no fair construction of my letter could authorize, so no approval by me could ratify the order, or its assignment.

Mr. President and Gentlemen,—I have, perhaps, passed over many things worthy of commentary; but this paper is already extended to an unreasonable length, and I feel satisfied that I have said all that is necessary for my defence. Reviewing my conduct now from the humiliating position in which I have been placed, I can not but still believe that, if I have fallen into any error, it is one which sprang from a kind and generous motive.

I submit my cause to you with entire confidence. Even if this 542
was a contest in which either the distinguished prosecutor or myself must fall, I should not doubt that you would administer even-handed justice, without respect to persons. But this is no

543 such case. Now that all the facts have been thoroughly ascertained, I trust that you are satisfied that so far as any statement made by me was understood to import more than the truth justifies, it was simply the result of misapprehension on one side or the other.

To you, Sir, and Gentlemen of the Court, I beg to return my
544 thanks for your patient attention during the trial, and to the Judge Advocate my acknowledgments of the courtesy and candor with which he has discharged his duty.

G. TALCOTT,
Bt. Brig. General, Colonel of Ordnance.

J. M. Carlisle, *of Counsel.*

www.ingramcontent.com/pod-product-compliance
Lightning Source LLC
LaVergne TN
LVHW021403110826
845150LV00007B/1772